ESL

ON COURSE 2

ON COURSE 2

student book

Jacqueline Flamm

Oxford University Press • 1989

Oxford University Press

200 Madison Avenue

New York, NY 10016 USA

Walton Street
Oxford OX2 6DP England

OXFORD is a trademark of Oxford University Press.

Library of Congress Cataloging-in-Publication Data

Flamm, Jacqueline, 1940-
   On Course 2. Student book.

   1.   English language—Textbooks for foreign speakers.
I.   Title. II.   Title: On Course two.
PE1128.F527 1989   428.3'4   89-8803
ISBN 0-19-434289-1
ISBN 0-19-434290-5 (Teacher's book)
ISBN 0-19-434291-3 (Cassettes)

Illustrations by Fernando Arteaga, Paulette Bogan, Adam Barr Brill, Jeff Faria, Marilyn Jones, Karin Kretschmann, Laura Hartman Maestro, Shelley Matheis, Andy Myer, S.D. Schindler, Arnie Ten, and Kurt Vargo.

Photographs and copyrighted images courtesy of Australian Tourist Commission; F. Bachrach/John F. Kennedy Library; British Tourist Authority; Canadian Consulate General; DC Comics Inc.; Owen Franken/Stock, Boston; French Government Tourist Office; Herman's World of Sporting Goods; Italian Government Travel Office; Japan Information Center, Consulate General of Japan, New York; Japan National Tourist Organization; Jeep; Denise J.H. Johnson; EP Jones/Camerique; Todd Kaplan/CBS Records, Inc.; Karsten Manufacturing Corp., makers of Ping golf clubs; Mark Kellogg; Don King Productions; Winnie Klotz/Metropolitan Opera; Llewellyn/Four by Five; Louisiana Superdome; Mike Mazzaschi/Stock, Boston; MCA Publishing, a Division of MCA Inc.; NASA; National Oceanic and Atmospheric Administration; Rob Nelson/Stock, Boston; New York Convention & Visitors Bureau; Paradise-Stitches; Peter Prench/Hawaii Visitors Bureau; Saks Fifth Avenue, New York; Ron Schramm/Chicago Convention & Visitors Bureau; Secretaria de Turismo de Mexico; Rena Seyfang; Sovfoto; Tass from Sovfoto; Travel Alberta; Universal Pictures, a Division of Universal City Studios, Inc.; and David Weintraub.

Studio photography by Cynthia Hill.
Location photography by Rhoda Sidney.

Graphics and realia by Alan Barnett, Maj-Britt Hagsted, David Halpern, and Stephen Van Litsenborg.

Picture research by Denise Johnson.

Cover design by Mark Kellogg.

Cover photo by Elizabeth Watt
Other photos by Bob Burch/Bruce Coleman, Inc. and Llewellyn/Four by Five.

Developmental Editor: Debbie Sistino
Editor: Lisa Ahlquist
Assistant Editor: Mary Sutherland

Senior Designer: Mark Kellogg
Art Researcher: Paula Radding

Printing (last digit): 10 9 8 7 6 5 4 3 2 1

Printed in Hong Kong

Preface

On Course is an easy-to-use, two-level speaking and listening course for young adults and adults who are beginning their study of English. Full-color, humorous illustrations and photographs support grammar and new vocabulary.

Both Books 1 and 2 follow a carefully sequenced grammatical syllabus and integrate communicative functions throughout. Topics include introductions, occupations, pastimes, shopping, transportation, restaurants, and everyday living.

The books are divided into 30 two-page units. Lessons have been developed so that they can be accomplished in 50-minute periods. Pair practice and information gap exercises provide many opportunities for student interaction. The six four-page summary units naturally recombine and reinforce the material that has been presented throughout the 30 units. A task listening activity is a regular feature of each summary unit.

The accompanying Teacher's Books are interleaved and include suggestions for presenting each lesson, a detailed syllabus, a word list, and a tapescript.

The Cassettes contain all of the dialogues and task listening sections in the Student Books.

Table of Contents

Unit		Page
1	What are you doing here?	2
2	Can you use a word processor?	4
3	Oh, what a toothache!	6
4	Can you show me those silk ties?	8
5	What are you going to do on Saturday?	10
Summary 1	Units 1–5	12
6	How was your vacation?	16
7	I like to watch ski jumping.	18
8	What'll you do if it rains?	20
9	There are 32 ounces in a quart.	22
10	There's a bedroom on the left.	24
Summary 2	Units 6–10	26
11	What were you doing last night?	30
12	I forgot to turn off the oven.	32
13	I think I look like my grandmother.	34
14	I always play poorly when I'm nervous.	36
15	Who's the best baseball player in the world?	38
Summary 3	Units 11–15	40
16	I was too tired to have a good time.	44
17	I've made a decision.	46
18	Have you ever visited Quebec?	48
19	I've been waiting since 12:00.	50
20	I'm so bored.	52
Summary 4	Units 16–20	54
21	You're from Chicago, aren't you?	58
22	He said he was very happy with my work.	60
23	I'm having my apartment painted.	62
24	What were you doing last night at 7:00?	64
25	I used to live in San Francisco.	66
Summary 5	Units 21–25	68
26	When do you expect to buy it?	72
27	Do you know what kind of gift you want?	74
28	I hope you can come.	76
29	Which newspaper do you usually read?	78
30	Who wrote Hamlet?	80
Summary 6	Units 26–30	82
Word and Phrase List		86

1

Listen to the conversation and practice with a partner.

A: Hi. *Is your brother* home?
B: No, *he's* on *his* way to *work*.
A: *Is he driving?*
B: Well, *he* usually *drives*, but today *he's taking the bus*.

Have similar conversations with a partner.

1. your husband
   New York
   fly
   take the train

2. your parents
   the office
   go by bus
   drive

3. Paula
   the supermarket
   drive
   walk

4. the kids/school
   walk
   take the bus

5. your wife/the city
   take the train
   drive

6. Jack/Florida
   drive
   fly

2

Listen to the conversation. Then work with a partner. Student A, form questions with the information in 1–4. Student B, find the people and answer the questions. Then Student B, ask questions with the information in 5–8. Student A, answer.

A: Who *always studies at home?*
B: *Wanda does.*

STUDENT A

1. always study at home
2. sometimes fly to Florida on vacation
3. always answer the telephone
4. often drive to Los Angeles

STUDENT B

5. always sleep late
6. usually take the train to work
7. always leave a message
8. usually walk to work

Joe   Sue and Art

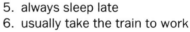

Lee   Robin

Wanda   Pete   Paul and Norman   Atsuko

3

Listen to the conversation and practice with a partner.

CAROL: Hi, Jack. What are you doing here?
JACK: Oh, hi. I'm buying an answering machine.
CAROL: Oh, really?
JACK: Yes, I always miss my phone calls because I'm never home in the evenings.
CAROL: What do you do?
JACK: Well, I *always see a movie on Sundays*. And *on Mondays...*

Have similar conversations with a partner to describe the rest of Jack's evenings. Use words from the chart.

always	*see a movie*	*on Sundays*
usually	work late	on Tuesdays (etc.)
often	visit friends	two evenings a week
sometimes	study in the library	every other evening
	eat out	
	go to a lecture	
	go to the gym	

4

Listen to the conversation and practice with a partner.

A: How do you usually go to work?
B: I usually take the bus. How do you go?
A: It depends. I often drive, but sometimes I ride my bike.
B: Do you ever take the bus?
A: Never.

Have similar conversations with a partner. Talk about where and how you go to school or work.

GRAMMAR					USEFUL LANGUAGE
I	always	study	at home.	Who usually drives to work?	What are you doing here?
He	often usually sometimes never	studies	on Tuesdays.		Oh, really? What do you do? On Sundays...
I'm He's They're	driving		today. now.		It depends. Do you ever take the bus?

1

Ms. Wright is conducting a job interview. Listen to the interview and practice with a partner.

MS. WRIGHT: Tell me, *Ms. Carter*, what languages do you speak?
MS. CARTER: My *Italian* is very good. And I speak a little Spanish.
MS. WRIGHT: Can you use a *word processor?*
MS. CARTER: Yes, I can.
MS. WRIGHT: Hmm. Do you have a driver's license?
MS. CARTER: Yes, I do. And I have a car.
MS. WRIGHT: *Good!* I have one more question. When can you begin?
MS. CARTER: Well, *immediately*, I guess.

Conduct similar interviews with a partner.

1. Mr. Amis
   Portugese
   a computer
   Great
   right away

2. Miss Yamaguchi
   Japanese
   a fax machine
   Excellent
   in two weeks

3. Mrs. Rizzo
   French
   a telex
   Wonderful
   Monday morning

4. Margo
   Russian
   an electronic
     typewriter
   Fine
   tomorrow

2

Listen to the conversation and practice with a partner.

JUDY: What kind of computer do you have?
BOB and JANE: *We* have *a Macintosh*.
JUDY: *Does* your *son* have *his* own computer?
BOB and JANE: Yes. *He has an Apple*.

Bob and Jane

Have similar conversations with a partner.

1. Joe
   IBM/brother
   Compaq

2. Sumio and Rose
   Leading Edge/
     daughter
   AT 200

3. Bill
   Hyundai/sister
   Macintosh

4. Ed and Pat
   Panasonic/children
   Epson

3

Practice this conversation with a partner. Talk about the people in 2.

A: Who has *an Apple?*
B: *Jane's son does*.

4

Listen to the conversation and practice with a partner.

A: Does Dave *type 50 words a minute?*
B: *No*, he *doesn't.*

B: Does Dave *have a driver's license?*
A: *Yes*, he *does.*

STUDENT A

NAME: _Dave Piermont_
STREET: _342 Glen Avenue_
CITY: _Rosemont_
STATE: _Ohio_
ZIP: _38638_
TELEPHONE: _(513) 478-2386_

	YES	NO
Driver's license:	☒	☐
Type 50 words a minute:	☐	☐
Familiarity with:		
Word processor	☐	☐
Electronic typewriter	☒	☐
Fax machine	☐	☒
Personal computer	☐	☐
Telex	☐	☐
Photocopier	☒	☐
Can you speak these languages?		
1. French	☐	☐
2. Italian	☐	☒
3. Japanese	☐	☐
4. Korean	☒	☐
5. Spanish	☐	☒

STUDENT B

NAME: _Dave Piermont_
STREET: _342 Glen Avenue_
CITY: _Rosemont_
STATE: _Ohio_
ZIP: _38638_
TELEPHONE: _(513) 478-2386_

	YES	NO
Driver's license:	☐	☐
Type 50 words a minute:	☐	☒
Familiarity with:		
Word processor	☒	☐
Electronic typewriter	☐	☐
Fax machine	☐	☐
Personal computer	☒	☐
Telex	☐	☒
Photocopier	☐	☐
Can you speak these languages?		
1. French	☒	☐
2. Italian	☐	☐
3. Japanese	☐	☒
4. Korean	☐	☐
5. Spanish	☐	☒

**Work with a partner. Student A, look at the job application on the left.
Student B, look at the job application on the right. Ask and answer
questions to complete your applications. Use the conversation.**

5

Now talk about Dave with another student. Use questions like these:

A: Does he have a driver's license?
B: Yes, he does.

GRAMMAR				USEFUL LANGUAGE
What kind of computer	do	you we they	have?	Tell me... My Italian is very good. Can you use a word processor?
	does	she he		Yes, I can. Does your son have his own computer?
Who has a Macintosh?	She does.			Ms.
	They do.			Mr.
				Mrs.
Do you speak Spanish?	Yes, I do./No, I don't.			Miss
Does he speak English?	Yes, he does./No, he doesn't.			

1

Listen to the conversation and practice with a partner.

ED: Oh, what a *toothache!* Ouch! This hurts!
SUE: You should go to the *dentist*.
ED: Well, it really isn't that *bad*.
SUE: It isn't *bad?* Then why are you *yelling?*
ED: I guess you're right. I should go to the *dentist* right away!
SUE: Well, go ahead! You'll feel better.

Have similar conversations with a partner.

1. stomachache
   emergency room
   terrible
   scream

2. backache
   doctor
   painful
   groan

3. headache
   eye doctor
   awful
   complain

4. sore throat
   clinic
   serious
   whisper

2

Listen to the conversation and practice with a partner.

SID: *Do I* have a fever?
DOCTOR: Yes, *you do*. It's 101°. It's probably the flu.
SID: Oh, no! *I have* to go to work tomorrow! *I have* an important meeting!
DOCTOR: *You* shouldn't go to work. *You* should stay in bed for a few days. And *you have* to take these pills three times a day.

Sid's friend, Pete, talks to Sid's mother.

PETE: May I speak to Sid, please?
MOTHER: No, I'm sorry, Sid is sick.
PETE: Does he have a fever?
MOTHER: Yes, he does. It's _____.

3

Listen to the conversation and practice with a partner.

A: *Mary has a terrible headache.* What should *she* do?

A: You're right. *She* should.

B: *She* should *take some aspirin.*

Work with a partner. Student A, ask Student B about the problem on the left. Student B, choose the best advice from the pictures on the right. Use the conversation.

STUDENT A: *PROBLEM*   STUDENT B: *ADVICE*

Joe/a bad stomachache

call the dentist

Reiko/a stuffy nose

see the doctor

He/a broken tooth

stop the bleeding

I/a bad cut

use some nasal spray

GRAMMAR				USEFUL LANGUAGE

I	have	to call the dentist.
He	has	

You	should stay in bed.
He	

What	should	I / he	do?

USEFUL LANGUAGE

Oh, what a toothache!
Ouch!
This hurts!
I guess you're right.
I should go right away.
Go ahead! You'll feel better.
You're right. She should.

1

Listen to the conversation and practice with a partner.

CUSTOMER: Excuse me. Can you *show* me
           those silk ties?
CLERK: Certainly. I'm busy now, but I'll
           show them to you in a minute.
CUSTOMER: Thank you. I'll wait.

this
that
these
those

**Have similar conversations with a partner. Ask about the items in the
chart. Substitute *give*, *hand*, and *bring* for *show*.**

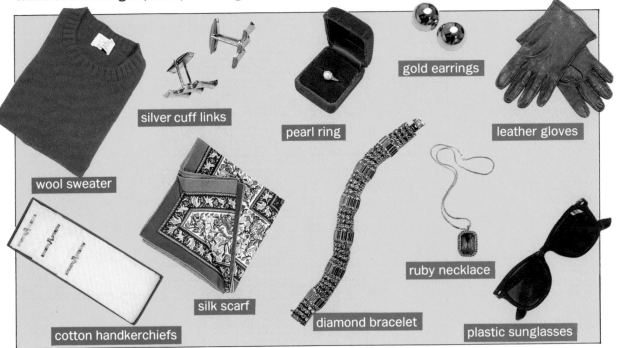

silver cuff links

gold earrings

pearl ring

leather gloves

wool sweater

ruby necklace

cotton handkerchiefs

silk scarf

diamond bracelet

plastic sunglasses

2

Listen to the conversation and practice with a partner.

A: Would you please *buy* me *a newspaper*?
B: Sure. I'll be happy to *buy* it *for* you.

Student A, ask Student B to do something for you. Then change parts.

Use *for* with these verbs: bake, buy, cook, find, get, make, type
Use *to* with these verbs: bring, give, read, send, show, tell

3

Listen to the conversation and practice with a partner.

A: I want to buy *a birthday* present for *your sister*.
B: You want to buy *her a birthday* present? You shouldn't!
A: But I want to. Tell me what *she wants*.
B: Well, OK. Get *her a videocassette*.
A: Great! I'll get *E.T.* for *her*.

Have similar conversations with a partner.

1. Christmas
   you
   clothes
   a sweater

2. Valentine's Day
   your daughter
   candy
   a chocolate heart

3. anniversary
   you and John
   flowers
   red roses

4. graduation
   William
   jewelry
   a gold watch

4

Listen to the conversations and practice with a partner.

A: What should I *give Sue* for *her birthday?*
B: *Give her a dress.*
A: Good idea! I'll *give* it to *her* tomorrow.

B: What should I *get the twins* for *their birthday?*
A: *Get them a TV.*
B: Good idea! I'll *get* it for *them* tomorrow.

Work with a partner. Student A, look at the chart on the left. Student B, look at the chart on the right. Ask and answer questions to fill in your charts. Use the conversation.

STUDENT A

	Christmas	Birthday	Graduation
give/Sue	scarf		
get/the twins		TV	books
buy/Joe		cake	

STUDENT B

	Christmas	Birthday	Graduation
give/Sue		dress	dictionary
get/the twins	dog		
buy/Joe	computer		watch

GRAMMAR	USEFUL LANGUAGE
Would you please [give / send / hand / buy / get] me a newspaper? I'll be happy to [give / send / hand / buy / get] it [to / for] you.	Excuse me. I'll wait. You shouldn't! But I want to. Good idea!

9

1

Listen to the conversation and practice with a partner.

PAULA: What *are you* going to do on Saturday?

TOM: *I have* a full day. First *I'm* going to *work out* at the health club. After that *I'm* probably going to *do my laundry*.

PAULA: What *are you* going to do then?

TOM: Well, *I'm* going to run six miles. *I'm* getting ready to run in the marathon next week.

PAULA: And then?

TOM: *I'm* not going to do anything after that. *I'm* going to be tired.

PAULA: I'm sure *you are!*

Have similar conversations with a partner.

1. Mike
    swim
    go shopping

2. your parents
    play racquetball
    have lunch

3. Alice
    lift weights
    visit her
    mother

4. your brothers
    take an
    aerobics class
    go to the
    supermarket

2

Listen to the conversation and practice with a partner.

TOM: *Are you* going to meet us at the Sleepy Crow after exercise class?

RAY: *I'm* exhausted. *I* can't move. *I'm* not going to meet *you*. *I'm* going to go straight home. First *I'm* going to turn on some music. Next *I'm* going to take a hot bath. After that *I'm* going to have a good dinner. Then *I'm* going to watch a movie on the VCR.

TOM: I think *you're* going to fall asleep during the movie.

RAY: You're probably right.

Alan is asking Tom about Ray. Work with a partner and finish the conversation.

ALAN: Is Ray going to meet us at the Sleepy Crow after exercise class?

TOM: He's exhausted. He can't move. He's _____.

3

Listen to the conversation and practice with a partner.

JOANIE: What *are you* going to do on Saturday?

BETTE: First *I'm* going to *clean my apartment.* Next *I'm* going to *work out at the health club.* Then *I'm* going to *get a haircut. I don't* know what *I'm* going to do after that, but one thing is certain. *I'm* not going to *do any work!*

Student A, ask Student B about Patrick and You and Sal. Student B, ask Student A about Rita and Tom and Janet.

STUDENT A

STUDENT B

Rita
sleep late
bake a cake
make a few phone calls
go to the office

Tom and Janet
wash the car
paint the bathroom
fix the roof
waste time

Patrick
wake up
eat something
go back to sleep
be tired

You and Sal
go to the video store
watch a few movies
go out to dinner
be bored

Work with a partner. Mention three things you are going to do next Saturday. Then mention one thing you are not going to do.

GRAMMAR		USEFUL LANGUAGE
First Next Then After that	I'm going to run six miles.	I have a full day. And then? I'm sure you are! I'm exhausted! I can't move! I'm going to go straight home. You're probably right.
I don't know what I'm going to do	first. next. then. after that.	

1

Look at the picture. Then listen and write the letter.

1. _k_   2. ____   3. ____   4. ____
5. ____   6. ____   7. ____   8. ____
9. ____   10. ____   11. ____   12. ____

2

Listen and write the letter of the best answer.

a. No, he's on his way to work.
(b.) No, he's taking the bus.

1. a. Maria does.
   b. Charles is.

2. a. I'm never home.
   b. I'm buying an answering machine.

3. a. I ride my bike.
   b. I usually study at home.

4. a. I speak Spanish and a little Italian.
   b. I can speak to you in the morning.

5. a. Oh, you shouldn't!
   b. But I want to.

6. a. We're going to be here on Thursday.
   b. We're going to do our laundry.

7. a. Yes, he has a computer.
   b. Yes, he has a Toyota.

8. a. No, I don't.
   b. Yes, he does.

9. a. She shouldn't go to work.
   b. She shouldn't go to the doctor.

10. a. Yes. He has to stay in bed.
    b. Yes. He has to call the dentist.

11. a. And then?
    b. I'm exhausted.

12. a. I'll be happy to buy it for you.
    b. I'll be glad to get them for you.

STUDENT A

3

Listen to the job interviews. Fill in the missing information. Circle "yes" or "no."

	Perry Jones	Rodney Taylor	Janice Forbes	Alice Rosen
RESUME	yes no	(yes) no	yes no	(yes) no
WORD PROCESSOR	yes (no)	yes no	(yes) no	yes no
TYPE	yes no	(yes) no	yes no	(yes) no
DRIVER'S LICENSE	yes (no)	yes no	(yes) no	yes no
LANGUAGES	_____	Spanish Italian	_____	Spanish French German
BEGIN	in a year	_____	immediately	_____

Check your answers with your partner. Ask about your missing information. Start like this:

A: Does Perry Jones have his resume?
B: No, he doesn't.

B: Can Perry Jones use a word processor?
A: No, he can't.

4

Student A, start the conversation. Then listen to your partner and choose a good answer. Continue the conversation. Then try the conversation again. Choose different answers.

—Hi, Joe. Is your sister home?

—What's she going to do after that?
—I think you should call the doctor for her.

—Is she going to be at the party tonight?
—Well, I'm driving to the drugstore. I'll be happy to get the medicine for her.

—Sure. Can I get anything else?
—Oh, well, I'm going to call her later.

STUDENT B

3

Listen to the job interviews. Fill in the missing information. Circle "yes" or "no."

	Perry Jones	Rodney Taylor	Janice Forbes	Alice Rosen
RESUME	yes (no)	yes no	yes (no)	yes no
WORD PROCESSOR	yes no	yes (no)	yes no	(yes) no
TYPE	yes (no)	yes no	(yes) no	yes no
DRIVER'S LICENSE	yes no	(yes) no	yes no	(yes) no
LANGUAGES	English	_____	Spanish French Russian	_____
BEGIN	_____	in a week	_____	in two weeks

Check your answers with your partner. Ask about your missing information. Start like this:

A: Does Perry Jones have his resume?
B: No, he doesn't.

B: Can Perry Jones use a word processor?
A: No, he can't.

4

Student B, listen to your partner and choose a good answer. Continue the conversation. Then try the conversation again. Choose different answers.

—Yes, but she has to stay in bed today. She has a fever.
—No, she isn't. She has a busy day today. First she's going to the health club.

—I think she has to do her laundry.
—I did. I have to get her some pills.

—I don't think so. She usually stays home on Saturday evenings.
—Thanks. Would you please get her some cough medicine, too?

—Yes. You can get a movie for the VCR.
—Good. I'm sure she's going to be here.

5

Ask and answer questions like this with a partner. Write your partner's answers.

A: What do you do *in the summer?*
B: I *always go to the beach. Sometimes I take a trip.*

_____ (name of partner)	always	usually	sometimes
in the spring on weekends on New Year's Eve after English class on Sunday mornings on Saturday evenings			

6

Work in a group of four or five. Find out the following information about the people in your group.

A: How many people *can use a word processor?*
B: I *can.*
C: I *can.*
D: I *can't.*
E: I *can't.*
A: And I *can't. Two* people *can use a word processor* and *three* people *can't.* or *Nobody can use a word processor.*

Have similar conversations with the following:

1. have a driver's license
2. can speak Spanish
3. own a car
4. can use a fax machine
5. have a computer
6. often have a cold

Report your results to the class.

1

Listen to the conversation and practice with a partner.

SARA: How was your vacation?
BETTY: It was great. First, we *flew* to *San Francisco*. Then we *took a cruise* to *Alaska*. When we got there we were exhausted. It took *two days* to get there.
SARA: What did you do all week?
BETTY: Oh, we did everything! We had delicious meals. We relaxed, and of course, we went *sightseeing*.
SARA: Sounds wonderful!

Have similar conversations with a partner.

1. fly/Miami
   take a cruise
   Puerto Rico
   two days
   swim in the ocean

2. drive
   British Columbia
   take a ferry
   Vancouver Island
   14 hours
   fish

3. drive/Point Judith
   take a ferry
   Block Island
   ten hours
   sail

4. take a train
   Washington, D.C.
   drive/Chesapeake
    Bay
   eight hours
   sail

5. drive/Los Angeles
   fly/Honolulu
   14 hours
   sightsee

6. take a boat
   St. Thomas
   fly/San Juan
   three days
   sail

2

Read Akio's diary about her trip to San Francisco. Then work with a partner and ask questions about her trip.

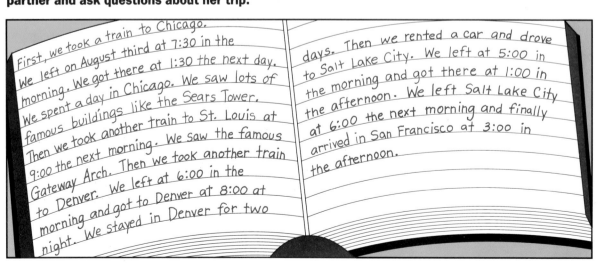

First, we took a train to Chicago. We left on August third at 7:30 in the morning. We got there at 1:30 the next day. We spent a day in Chicago. We saw lots of famous buildings like the Sears Tower. Then we took another train to St. Louis at 9:00 the next morning. We saw the famous Gateway Arch. Then we took another train to Denver. We left at 6:00 in the morning and got to Denver at 8:00 at night. We stayed in Denver for two days. Then we rented a car and drove to Salt Lake City. We left at 5:00 in the morning and got there at 1:00 in the afternoon. We left Salt Lake City at 6:00 the next morning and finally arrived in San Francisco at 3:00 in the afternoon.

3

Work with a partner. Student A, look at map A and ask Student B about his/her trip. Student B, look at map B and answer the questions that Student A asks you.

STUDENT A

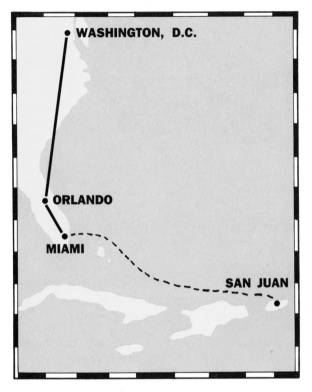

STUDENT B

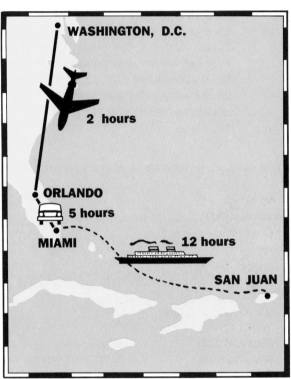

When was your vacation?
How did you get from _____ to _____?
How long did it take?
When did you leave?

Last month
Plane departed: March 11, 11:00 A.M.
      arrived: March 11, 1:00 P.M.
  Car departed: March 13, 9:00 A.M.
      arrived: March 13, 2:00 P.M.
Boat departed: March 14, 6:00 P.M.
      arrived: March 15, 6:00 A.M.

4

Work with a partner and talk about a trip you took.

fly	flew	leave	left	do	did
take	took	eat	ate	spend	spent
drive	drove	go	went	see	saw
get	got	have	had	is	was/were

GRAMMAR							USEFUL LANGUAGE
We	flew	to San Francisco.		Did		drive?	Sounds wonderful!
	took	a train.	What	did	you	do?	How long did it take?
	left	at 10:00.	When			leave?	How did you get from _____ to _____?

1

Listen to the conversation and practice with a partner.

LAURA: Can *you* come over tonight? We're going to watch *the Winter Olympics* on TV.
LIZ: It sounds like fun.
LAURA: I like to watch *ski jumping*.
LIZ: I like to watch it, too. I could *ski* years ago, but I'm not very good at it now. What about you?
LAURA: Oh, I was never able to *ski* well. I couldn't *stay on my feet!*

Have similar conversations with a partner.

1. you and Bob
   Ice Capades
   ice skating
   skate
   keep my balance

2. you
   Summer Olympics
   swimming
   swim
   stay afloat

3. Andrew
   World Series
   baseball
   play softball
   hit the ball

4. you and your family
   Wimbledon
   tennis
   play
   see the ball

2

Listen to the conversation and practice with a partner.

A: Could you *play tennis* when you were a child?
B: No, I couldn't.
A: Were you able to *roller skate* when you were a child?
B: Yes, I was.

Work with a partner. Student A, look at the chart on the left. Student B, look at the chart on the right. Ask and answer questions to finish your charts. Use the conversations.

STUDENT A

	Jack	Sue	Dave and Kevin
Roller skate		no	
Play tennis	no		no
Ice skate		no	
Bowl	no		yes
Ski		yes	
Swim	yes		yes

STUDENT B

	Jack	Sue	Dave and Kevin
Roller skate	yes		yes
Play tennis		no	
Ice skate	yes		yes
Bowl		no	
Ski	no		no
Swim		yes	

Now ask a partner the same questions using other sports.

3

Listen to the conversation and practice with a partner.

A: What *does your husband* like to do on weekends?

B: *He likes* to *watch football*.

Have similar conversations with a partner.

1. you
   run

2. Judy and Keiko
   play tennis

3. your friends
   go bowling

4. you and Shirley
   watch baseball

5. your mother
   garden

6. your children
   swim

7. you and Jack
   cook

8. Bob
   play cards

Student A, ask what sport Student B likes to do on vacation. Ask if Student B does the activity well. Ask about Student B's family. Then change parts.

A: What sport *do you* like to do on vacation?

B: *I like* to *play golf*.

A: *Can you play* well?

B: Yes, *I can.*/No, *I can't. I was* never able to *play* well.

GRAMMAR								USEFUL LANGUAGE
Are	you	able to	ski	now?	Yes,	I he she it	can. could.	Can you come over tonight? It sounds like fun. What about you?
Can								
Were	you	able to	ski	when you	No,	we you they	can't. couldn't.	
Could				were a child?				
He likes to watch football.								

1 **Listen to the conversation and practice with a partner.**

MOLLY: What *are you* doing next Sunday?
BOB: It depends on the weather. *I* may *take some pictures* unless it rains.
MOLLY: What'll *you* do if it rains?
BOB: I guess *I'll develop some film*.

Have similar conversations with a partner.

1. Jerry
    go out
    stay home

2. you and Chuck
    play golf
    go bowling

3. your children
    play baseball
    watch movies on
    the VCR

4. Barbara
    go sailing
    work at home

2 **Work with a partner. Student A, look at the chart on the left. Student B, look at the chart on the right. Ask and answer questions about what different people are doing next weekend, depending on the weather. Use the conversation in 1.**

STUDENT A

Thomas		
Peter and Jack	play tennis	play cards
you and Marta		
Samuel	ride his bike	read a book
your parents		
Molly and Danny		
you and I	work in the garden	write some letters

STUDENT B

Thomas	go to Boston	work at home
Peter and Jack		
you and Marta	have a picnic	clean the house
Samuel		
your parents	go to the beach	go to the library
Molly and Danny	go swimming	go to the movies
you and I		

3

Listen to the conversation and practice with a partner.

BARRY: Dinner's ready and *Joan isn't* here. I wonder where *she is*.

LOU: Well, the weather's awful. *She* might still be *at work*.

Have similar conversations with a partner.

1. Carol and Linda
   at school

2. your mother
   on the road

3. your uncle
   on the bus

4. Mr. and Mrs. Block
   at home

4

Listen to the conversation and practice with a partner.

MARK: How *are you* doing?

GEORGE: *I'm* not doing very well. I think *I* might *fail the French course*.

MARK: I'm sorry to hear it. If *you do*, will *you go to summer school*?

GEORGE: *I* might. *I'm* not sure yet.

Have similar conversations with a partner.

1. Julie
   lose her job
   stay in town

2. your brother
   need an operation
   miss a lot of
   work

3. you
   work on Sunday
   take Monday
   off

4. your parents
   sell their house
   buy another one

GRAMMAR	USEFUL LANGUAGE
I may / might take some pictures unless it rains.	It depends on the weather.
What'll you do if it rains?	I wonder where she is.
I'll stay home if it rains.	The weather's awful.
	I'm not doing very well.
	I'm sorry to hear it.
	I might.
	I'm not sure yet.

1

Listen to the conversation and practice with a partner.

LISA: How much *milk* do you want?
MOM: *A half-gallon*.
LISA: Hey, Mom, do you know how many ounces are in *a half-gallon?*
MOM: Oh, that's easy. Let's see. There are *32* ounces in a *quart*, so there are *64* ounces in *a half-gallon*.
LISA: Right. Pretty good, Mom.

Have similar conversations with a partner.

1. cheese
   two pounds

2. coffee
   three pounds

3. juice
   one gallon

4. butter
   one half pound

LIQUID MEASURES	ABBREVIATIONS
1 cup = 8 ounces	oz. = ounce
1 pint = 2 cups	pt. = pint
1 quart = 2 pints	qt. = quart
1 gallon = 4 quarts	gal. = gallon
1 liter = 1.057 quarts	lb. = pound
DRY MEASURES	g = gram
1 pound = 16 ounces	L = liter
1 gram = .035 ounces	

2

Listen to the conversation and practice with a partner.

ROY: What can I pick up at the store?
BRIAN: Well, we need some *tuna fish*.
ROY: How *much* do you want?
BRIAN: Get *a large can*.

ROY: What can I pick up at the store?
BRIAN: Well, we need some *yogurt*.
ROY: How *many containers* do you want?
BRIAN: Get *one large container*.

Have similar conversations with a partner.

1. cereal
   a large box

2. soda
   one bottle

3. tomato sauce
   a small can

4. candy
   two large bags

3

Listen to the conversation and practice with a partner.

BARBARA: We should make a list of things to buy for the *party*. How many people are coming?
GAIL: About *20*. We'll need a lot of *soda*.
BARBARA: Get *ten liters*, and get some *juice*, too.
GAIL: OK. I'll get *four quarts*. We don't have any *cheese*. I'll get *three pounds*. I'll go now.

PARTY FOR 20 PEOPLE
10 liters soda
4 qts. juice
3 lbs. cheese

Have similar conversations with a partner.

1. reception/50
   tea/three boxes
   coffee/four pounds
   cookie/eight pounds

2. picnic/15
   soda/six liters
   wine/five bottles
   potato chips/six bags

3. bridal shower/30
   soda/ten six-packs
   juice/three quarts
   cheese/four pounds

4. party/12
   crackers/seven boxes
   beer/five six-packs
   cream cheese/two pounds

4

Below is a list of food found in your kitchen.
Work with a partner and decide what you will
need for a party. Use the conversation.

LIST

1 qt. milk	1/4 lb. pasta
no sauce	3 pieces of bread
no sugar	1 lb. coffee
no cake	6 tea bags
a little salad	1 box cookies (half-full)
a few potato chips	5 crackers in box
a can of beer	1/4 lb. cheese
no wine	1 bottle juice (half-full)
2 pieces of chicken	no soda

STUDENT A: Do we need any soda?
STUDENT B: Yes. There's no soda left. Let's
get _____.
STUDENT A: Do we need any juice?
STUDENT B: Yes. There's a little juice. Let's
get _____.
STUDENT A: How much pasta should we buy?
STUDENT B: Well, there's only a little left.
Let's buy _____.
STUDENT A: How much chicken do we need?
STUDENT B: Well, there are only two pieces,
so we should get _____.

5

Work with a partner and plan a party for your friends. First, decide
what you will serve, and then make a list of the food you need.

GRAMMAR								USEFUL LANGUAGE
How	much	milk	do you want?	Is	there	any	cheese?	That's easy.
	many	quarts		Are			cookies?	Let's see.
								Right.
We need	some	yogurt.		There	is	some.		Pretty good.
	a lot of	cookies.				none.		What can I pick up
						no sugar.		at the store?
We need a little yogurt.								How many people
					are	no cookies.		are coming
								to the party?
We don't need any	yogurt.				aren't	any.		
	cookies.							

23

1

Pat wants to sell her house. She's showing it to Amy. Listen to the conversation and practice with a partner.

AMY: What a nice house you have!
PAT: Thank you.
AMY: This is a nice *kitchen*. What's through that door?
PAT: Oh, that's the *living room*
AMY: Where *are the bedrooms?*
PAT: One *bedroom* is *next to the den* and the other one is *upstairs*.

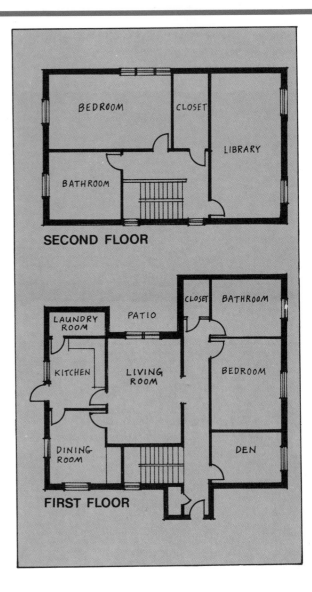

SECOND FLOOR

FIRST FLOOR

Have similar conversations with a partner.

1. living room
   kitchen
   bathrooms
   next to that
     bedroom
   upstairs

2. dining room
   kitchen
   bedrooms
   across from the
     living room
   upstairs

3. den
   living room
   bedrooms
   through that door
   upstairs

4. bedroom
   closet
   bathrooms
   through that door
   downstairs

5. library
   bathroom
   closets
   next to that
     bedroom
   downstairs

6. laundry room
   kitchen
   bedrooms
   next to the den
   upstairs

2

Listen to Amy talk about the house.

"Oh, it's just beautiful. First, you walk in and on the left is the living room. At the end of the living room is the dining room. You walk through the living room to get to the kitchen. The kitchen is great! There's a beautiful new sink. There are brand new cabinets above the sink. Under the sink there are enough cabinets to fit all of my pots and pans. Oh, and in the corner of the kitchen there's a huge window. There are two bedrooms. One bedroom is on the right as you walk in. The other one is upstairs. Then there's a bathroom next to each bedroom. And there's a huge closet downstairs and another one upstairs. There's a laundry room next to the kitchen. And there's a library upstairs across from the bedroom. It's a great place to live!"

Now work with a partner and practice asking and answering questions about the house.

Use questions like these: How many bedrooms are there?
                         Where are the cabinets?
                         Is there a dining room?

3

Look at the floor plans and listen to the description. Choose the correct floor plan.

There's a bedroom on the left. Next to the bedroom is the bathroom. On the right is the living room. The kitchen is through the living room.

Now work with a partner and describe the other floor plans.

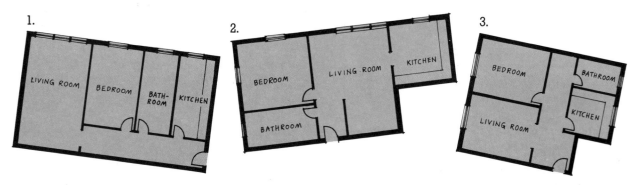

1. LIVING ROOM BEDROOM BATH-ROOM KITCHEN

2. BEDROOM LIVING ROOM KITCHEN BATHROOM

3. BEDROOM BATHROOM LIVING ROOM KITCHEN

4

Listen to the conversation and practice with a partner.

MOVER:	Where do you want the bed?
WOMAN:	Put the bed on the right wall.
MOVER:	Where do you want the dresser?
WOMAN:	Put the dresser opposite the bed.
MOVER:	How about the mirror?
WOMAN:	Put the mirror above the dresser.
MOVER:	What about this rocking chair?
WOMAN:	Put that in the corner.
MOVER:	Where does the table go?
WOMAN:	That goes under the window.
MOVER:	And the bookcase?
WOMAN:	That should go opposite the window, against the wall.
MOVER:	And the nightstands?
WOMAN:	They go on either side of the bed.

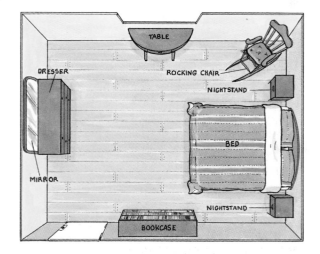

With your partner, decide where the items can go.

| ITEMS | box | picture | PLACE | on the wall | under the bed |
| | lamp | plant | | on the table | in the right corner |

GRAMMAR		USEFUL LANGUAGE
There's a beautiful kitchen.	through the door	What a nice house you have!
Is there a dining room?	next to the window	There are enough cabinets to fit everything.
There are two bedrooms.		It's a great place to live.
How many bedrooms are there?	in the corner	Where do you want the bed?
on the right / the wall	opposite / on either side of / the bed	
under / above / the sink	The other one is / upstairs. / downstairs.	

1

Listen and circle the letter of the best answer.

a. Of course.
(b.) It was great.
c. Sounds wonderful!

1. a. Yes, I do.
   b. One half pound.
   c. Two quarts.

2. a. It depends on the weather.
   b. We did everything.
   c. Pretty good.

3. a. I'm not sure yet.
   b. He's sorry to hear it.
   c. He might still be at the office.

4. a. She relaxed and went sightseeing.
   b. She likes to watch TV.
   c. She's going to watch the Summer Olympics on TV.

5. a. Yes, I could.
   b. Yes, they could.
   c. No, we couldn't.

6. a. They play softball.
   b. They're going to watch movies on the VCR.
   c. I may play golf. It depends on the weather.

7. a. About 20.
   b. Get a large container.
   c. Get a large can of tomato sauce.

8. a. Put it in the refrigerator.
   b. They go on either side of the bed.
   c. Put it next to the bed.

9. a. Oh, that's the patio.
   b. It's next to the living room.
   c. This is a nice kitchen.

10. a. I guess I'll stay home.
    b. Yes, I do, unless it rains.
    c. They're going to go roller skating.

11. a. I might. I'm not sure yet.
    b. I'm not doing very well.
    c. If I do, I'll go to work.

12. a. No, I couldn't.
    b. No, I wasn't.
    c. No, I'm not.

2

Look at the pictures. Listen to three sentences about each picture. Circle the letter of the best sentence.

1. a (b) c

2. a b c

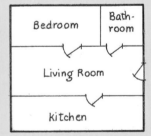

3. a b c

4. a b c

5. a b c

6. a b c

7. a b c

8. a b c

Work with a partner for Parts 3 and 4. Student A, look at this page. Student B, look at the next page.

STUDENT A

3

Listen to the conversation between Janice and Peter.

Listen again. Write in the names of the rooms on the floor plan.

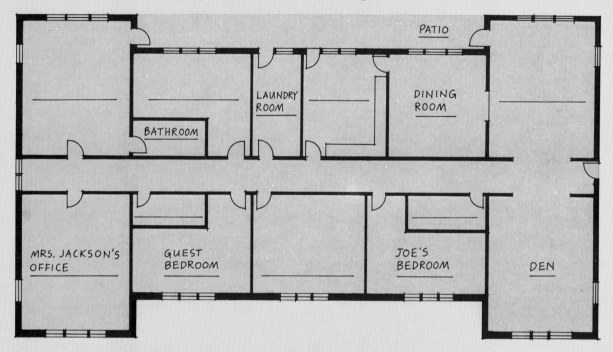

Check your answers with your partner. Start like this:

A: Where's the living room?
B: It's on the right as you walk in.
A: How many bathrooms are there?
B: There are three. One bathroom is on the left as you walk in. It's between the den and Joe's bedroom. Another one . . .

Use words like: through, next to, the other, opposite, against, on the right/left.

4

Student A, start the conversation. Then listen to your partner and choose a good answer. Continue the conversation. Then try the conversation again. Choose different answers.

—What are you doing next Saturday?

—What'll you do if it rains?
—It sounds like fun. How many people are coming?

—Oh, I was never able to bowl well. I couldn't keep my balance.
—Sure. How much do you need?

—Maybe the weather will be good.
—OK. Is that it?

—Well, I hope you have a good time with whatever you do!
—No problem. I can pick everything up for you Saturday afternoon.

STUDENT B

3

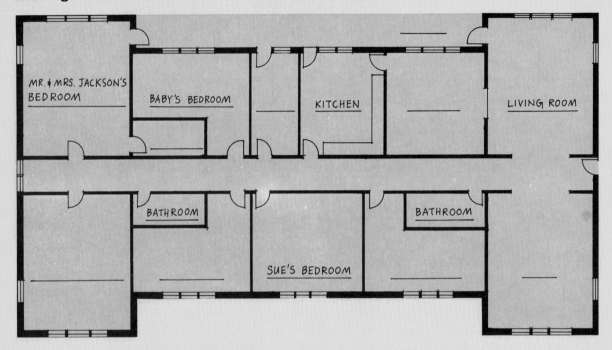

Listen to the conversation between Janice and Peter.

Listen again. Write in the names of the rooms on the floor plan.

MR. & MRS. JACKSON'S BEDROOM

BABY'S BEDROOM

KITCHEN

LIVING ROOM

BATHROOM

BATHROOM

SUE'S BEDROOM

Check your answers with your partner. Start like this:

A: Where's the living room?
B: It's on the right as you walk in.
A: How many bathrooms are there?
B: There are three. One bathroom is on the left as you walk in. It's between the den and Joe's bedroom. Another one...

Use words like: through, next to, the other, opposite, against, on the right/left.

4

Student B, listen to your partner and choose a good answer. Continue the conversation. Then try the conversation again. Choose different answers.

—I may take a drive in the country unless it rains.
—I'm having a party. Can you come?

—About 30. Can you pick up some soda at the store for me?
—Well, I may go bowling.

—About three liters. Oh, and two large bags of potato chips.
—Well, I'm not very good at it.

—Right. Then I can go for a drive.
—No. I need two pounds of coffee and two pounds of cheese.

5

Take a piece of paper. In ten minutes, make as many sentences as you can about doing things in the future. Choose words and phrases from 1, 2, 3, 4, 5, and 6.

         1   2   3   4 5   6
Mr. and Mrs. Raker will take a cruise to Alaska in January.

 1   2   3   4   5   6
Elliot might ride a bicycle through Paris this year.

1. Mr. and Mrs. Raker
   I
   Elliot

   My grandparents
   you
   Nancy

   _____
   (name of student)

2. will
   be going to

   want to
   may/might

3. take a cruise   take a train
   drive   ride a bicycle
   fly   sail

   swim
   go sightseeing

4. to
   in

   through
   on

5. Alaska
   the Canary Islands
   Paris

   Spain
   the Caribbean
   the beach

6. in January
   next week
   this year

   tomorrow
   tonight
   for a month

Work in teams. A student from Team A says a sentence. It must be a good sentence in English. Then a student from Team B says a different sentence. Continue until one team can't make any more new sentences.

1

Listen to the conversation and practice with a partner.

BRAD: What *were you* doing last night?
EILEEN: *I was* watching *a movie—New York Law Court*.
BRAD: Did *you like* it?
EILEEN: *I liked* most of it, but not all of it.

Have similar conversations with a partner.

1. Jack
   a documentary
   The Desert
   enjoy

2. you and Toby
   a French film
   La Nuit
   understand

3. Gary and Molly
   a concert
   The Boston Pops
   record

4. Aunt Helen
   an opera
   Faust
   love

2

Listen to the conversation and practice with a partner.

LAWYER: Where did *Mr. Gibb* go on *Wednesday evening?*
WITNESS: *He* went to *the library*.
LAWYER: What *was he* doing there?
WITNESS: *He was reading a book about poison*.
LAWYER: I see. And *was he* living in New York *a year* ago?
WITNESS: I think *he was*. Yes, I'm sure *he was*.

Have similar conversations with a partner.

1. Mrs. Pearson
   Saturday night
   a party
   talk to Mr. Samson
   five years

2. John and Rob Brown
   Sunday morning
   the park
   bury something
   seven weeks

3. you
   Thursday evening
   the gym
   take an aerobics
     class
   eighteen months

4. you and your
     husband
   Monday morning
   the mall
   buy luggage
   six months

3

Student A, ask where Student B went on a particular day and what he/she was doing. Use the conversation in 2. Then change parts.

4

Listen to the conversation and practice with a partner.

A: Where *were you living in 1968?*
B: *I was living* in *Osaka.*

**Have similar conversations with a partner.
Use this information.**

you		in 1987
your family		in January
your wife/husband		a year ago
your mother/father	work	a few years ago
your daughter/son		two months
your children		last year
your aunt/uncle	study	yesterday

5

Listen to the conversation and practice with a partner.

A: What *were you* doing when I called?
B: *I was taking a nap.*

**Work with a partner. Student A, ask Student B what Jane, Robert, and
Karen and Paul were doing when you called. Student B, ask Student A
what Alice, James, and the twins were doing when you called. Use the
conversation.**

STUDENT A   ## STUDENT B

GRAMMAR							USEFUL LANGUAGE
What	was	I / he	doing last night?	Yes,	he was. / we were.		I liked most of it, but not all of it.
	were	you / they		No,	he wasn't. / we weren't.		I think he was.
I	was	watching a movie.		What	was he / were you	doing when I called?	Yes, I'm sure he was.
They	were						
Was	he	living in New York	last month?				
Were	you		a year ago? / in 1968.				

1

Listen to the conversation and practice with a partner.

A: Hello?
B: Hi. Listen, could you do me a favor?
A: Sure.
B: I forgot to *turn off the oven*.
A: You forgot to *turn the oven off?*
B: Uh, yes.
A: Relax. I'll *turn it off* as soon as I hang up the phone.
B: Thanks. I was really worried.

> For animals use he or she.

Have similar conversations with a partner.

1. let out
   the cat

2. hang up
   the laundry

3. take out
   the garbage

4. pick up
   my shirts

5. turn off
   your computer

6. put away
   the food

7. turn off
   the iron

8. take out
   the dog

2

Listen to the conversation and practice with a partner.

MOTHER: Would you do a few things for me while I'm gone?
PATRICK: Sure, Mom.
MOTHER: First, *straighten up the living room*. Then *throw out* the *newspapers*, *pick up* the *toys*, and *clean out* the *closet*.
PATRICK: OK. I'll *straighten* the *living room up*, *throw* the *newspapers out, pick* the *toys up*, and *clean* the *closet out*. Anything else?
MOTHER: Yes. After that, why don't you *call up* one of your friends and go to a movie?
PATRICK: Mom, after that I'll be so tired I'll have to go to bed!

Now look at the To Do List and have similar conversations with a partner.

To Do List			
LIVING ROOM	BEDROOM	KITCHEN	BATHROOM
straighten up	clean up	clean up	clean up
throw out newspapers	hang up clothes	throw away leftovers	wash out shower
pick up toys	put away laundry	wash off counters	put away towels
clean out closet	take off sheets	take out garbage	wipe off sink

3

Listen to the interview and practice with a partner.

INTERVIEWER: Excuse me. I'm from **House** magazine. Would you mind answering a few questions about household chores? Who does the housework in your house?

SHOPPER: We all pitch in.

INTERVIEWER: I see. Who does the cooking?

SHOPPER: *I don't* like to cook. *My husband makes* dinner. We make our own breakfast and lunch. *I do* the dishes.

INTERVIEWER: Who makes the beds?

SHOPPER: We make our own beds.

INTERVIEWER: And the *laundry*?

SHOPPER: I do the *laundry*.

INTERVIEWER: Well, thank you very much. Excuse me. I'm from . . .

Have similar conversations with a partner.

1. my wife/I
   she
   dusting

2. my roommate/I
   the dishwasher
   vacuuming

3. I/my husband
   our son
   cleaning

4. my wife and I/our
   daughter
   she
   shopping

Use *make* with these words:
the beds   breakfast   lunch
dinner   the decisions

Use *do* with these words:
the chores   the dishes   the housework
the dusting   the laundry

4

Bill's friend, Sam, is going to help him clean his apartment. Look at the picture below and decide what to tell Sam to do. Work with a partner and practice the conversation.

BILL: Could you please *pick up all the newspapers?*

SAM: Sure, I'll *pick them up*.

BILL: Could you please *put away the clothes?*

SAM: Sure, I'll *put them away*.

GRAMMAR		USEFUL LANGUAGE
Turn off the oven.	He makes the beds.	Could you do me a favor?
Turn the oven off.	She does the dishes.	Relax.
Turn it off.		Would you do a few things for me?
Pick up the newspapers.		Would you mind answering a few questions?
Pick the newspapers up.		We all pitch in.
Pick them up.		

1

Listen to the conversation and practice with a partner.

STEVE: *Pete, who is that woman* over there?
PETE: *That's* my *aunt, Sue.*
STEVE: I think you look like *her!*
PETE: Really? I don't think so. I think I look like my *brother, Joe.*

Have similar conversations with a partner.

1. Paul
   woman
   sister
   mother

2. Jennifer
   man
   grandfather
   brother

3. Joe
   people
   parents
   grandmother

4. Adam
   boys
   cousins
   sister

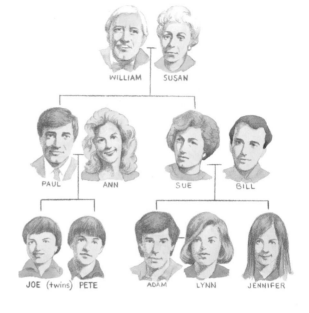

WILLIAM   SUSAN

PAUL   ANN   SUE   BILL

JOE (twins) PETE   ADAM   LYNN   JENNIFER

2

Listen to the conversations and practice with a partner.

A: Who *do you* look like in *your* family?
B: I think *I look* like *my grandmother.*

A: Who *does your wife* look like in *her* family?
B: I think *she looks* like *her brother.*

Ask your partner if he/she resembles anyone in his/her family. Then ask about sisters, brothers, children, spouses, cousins, and so on.

3

Listen to the conversation and practice with a partner.

A: What *are you* doing this Saturday afternoon?
B: *I have* to do some errands.
A: *You don't* look very happy about it.
B: *I'm* not. *I have* to take *my cousin* with *me.*
A: What's wrong with that?
B: Well, *I* don't get along with *him.*
A: Maybe *he* won't show up.
B: Not a chance.

Have similar conversations with a partner.

1. Bob
   nephew

2. you and Jay
   nieces

3. you
   mother-in-law

4. Samantha
   brother

5. your brothers
   little cousins

6. Alicia
   nephews

7. you
   sisters

8. you and Nancy
   aunt

4

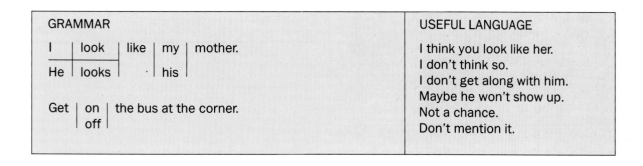

Listen to the conversation and practice with a partner.

SHOPPER 1: Excuse me. I want to go to the *post office* on *Gordon Avenue*. Can you tell me how to get there?

SHOPPER 2: Sure. Get on the *Woods Avenue* bus at the corner of *Woods* and *Penn*. Get off the bus at *Long Street*. Walk a few blocks *north* to *Gordon Avenue*.

SHOPPER 1: Thanks a lot.

SHOPPER 2: Don't mention it.

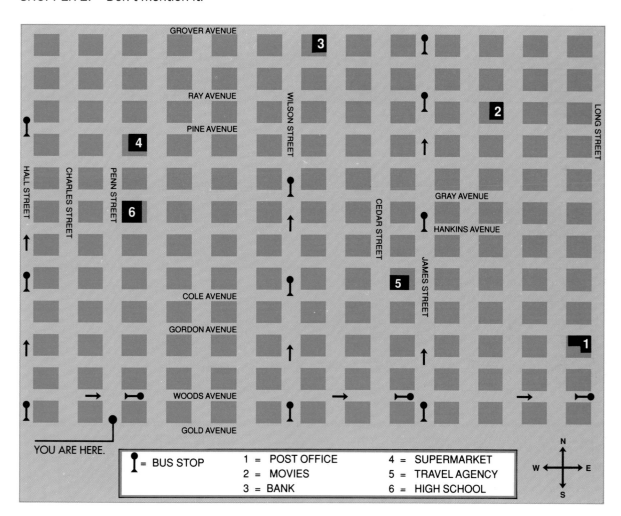

Have similar conversations with a partner. Use the map and ask about the bank, the movie theater, the supermarket, the travel agency, and so on.

GRAMMAR						USEFUL LANGUAGE
I	look	like	my	mother.		I think you look like her.
He	looks	·	his			I don't think so.
						I don't get along with him.
Get	on	the bus at the corner.				Maybe he won't show up.
	off					Not a chance.
						Don't mention it.

1

Listen to the conversation and practice with a partner.

A: I'm so glad it's Friday. What are you going to do this weekend?
B: I guess I'll spend the weekend *playing tennis*.
A: Oh, yeah? Are you a good *tennis player?*
B: I don't *play* very *well*. But I just love *playing tennis*. It relaxes me.

1. swim
   swimmer
   well

2. run
   runner
   fast

3. knit
   knitter
   carefully

4. read
   reader
   quickly

2

Listen to the conversation and practice with a partner.

A: How did your *piano lesson* go?
B: The *lesson* went well, but I *played* badly.
A: How come?
B: I was nervous. I always *play* poorly when I'm nervous.

1. tennis lesson
   play

2. painting class
   paint

3. skiing lesson
   ski

4. swimming class
   swim

5. dance class
   dance

6. singing lesson
   sing

3

Listen to the joke and practice with your partner.

A: How do you *feed a lion?*
B: *Quickly!*

Now practice other jokes with a partner.

1. pick up a snake
   carefully

2. eat a terrible dinner
   fast

4

Look at the evaluation form and then listen to the conversation. Practice with a partner.

WORK EVALUATION FORM	POOR	GOOD	EXCELLENT	COMMENT
Following directions	✓			Doesn't listen carefully
Answering phones			✓	Speaks very politely
Typing		✓		Very fast
Writing reports	✓			Writes carelessly
Writing memos		✓		Writes slowly, but accurately

MS. HASKEL: Good morning, Joanne. Are you ready to have your annual work evaluation? There's good news and bad news. First, what do you think is your weak point?

JOANNE: I guess *following directions* is my weak point.

MS. HASKEL: Yes, Joanne. *Following directions* is a very important skill.

JOANNE: Yes, I agree. And what about my *writing?*

MS. HASKEL: You *write your reports very carelessly.* You *write memos accurately,* but *very slowly.*

JOANNE: But my *typing* is good.

MS. HASKEL: Yes, Joanne, you *type* very *fast.* And you *speak very politely* on the phone. You always speak *clearly* and *carefully.* And I know that you work very hard.

JOANNE: Yes, I do. I'll try to do better in the future.

With a partner, fill out an evaluation form like the one above. Take the parts of Ms. Haskel and Joanne. Use the conversation.

IRREGULAR ADVERBS	
Adjective	*Adverb*
good	well
hard	hard
fast	fast

OPPOSITES	
fast, quickly	slowly
well	badly, poorly
accurately	inaccurately
politely	impolitely
carefully	carelessly

GRAMMAR			USEFUL LANGUAGE
I love	playing tennis. swimming.	He's a good tennis player. He plays tennis well.	I'm so glad it's Friday. It relaxes me.
Playing tennis Swimming	relaxes me.	She's a slow writer. She writes slowly.	How come? (Why?) I'll try to do better.

1

Listen to the conversation and practice with a partner.

MARLA: Would you like to play Geographical Trivia?

DONNY: Sure. You start.

MARLA: OK. Which is *higher, Mt. Everest* or *Mt. McKinley?*

DONNY: Let me see...*Mt. Everest* is *higher* than *Mt. McKinley*.

MARLA: Is *Mt. Everest* the *highest mountain* in the world?

DONNY: Yes, I believe it is.

Have similar conversations with a partner.

1. large
   the Pacific
   the Atlantic
   ocean

2. long
   the Nile
   the Amazon
   river

3. tall
   Angel Falls
   Tegula Falls
   waterfall

4. big
   Greenland
   New Guinea
   island

5. deep
   Lake Superior
   Lake Michigan
   lake

6. large
   the Sahara
   the Gobi
   desert

7. less populated
   Antarctica
   Oceania
   continent

8. more populated
   Asia
   Africa
   continent

Continue playing Geographical Trivia with a partner. Ask about other geographical facts. Use an almanac or encyclopedia to check your facts.

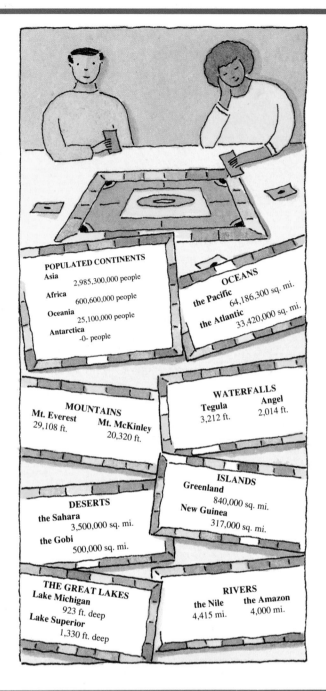

POPULATED CONTINENTS
Asia   2,985,300,000 people
Africa   600,600,000 people
Oceania   25,100,000 people
Antarctica -0- people

OCEANS
the Pacific 64,186,300 sq. mi.
the Atlantic 33,420,000 sq. mi.

MOUNTAINS
Mt. Everest 29,108 ft.   Mt. McKinley 20,320 ft.

WATERFALLS
Tegula 3,212 ft.   Angel 2,014 ft.

ISLANDS
Greenland 840,000 sq. mi.
New Guinea 317,000 sq. mi.

DESERTS
the Sahara 3,500,000 sq. mi.
the Gobi 500,000 sq. mi.

THE GREAT LAKES
Lake Michigan 923 ft. deep
Lake Superior 1,330 ft. deep

RIVERS
the Nile 4,415 mi.   the Amazon 4,000 mi.

2

Listen to the conversation and practice with a partner.

SUE: Excuse me. I think *those are our seats.* Yes, I'm sure *they're ours.*

MAN: *They are?* Yes, you're right. *They're yours.* I'm sorry.

SUE: No problem.

Have similar conversations with a partner.

1. my/raincoat   2. his/briefcase   3. their/shopping bags   4. her/pocketbook

3

Listen to the conversation and practice with a partner.

SUE: Who *writes more clearly, Anne* or *Sal?*
DAVE: *Sal writes more clearly* than *Anne*. In fact, *Sal writes the most clearly* of all.

Have similar conversations with a partner.

1. drive/carefully

2. dress/beautifully

3. sing/badly

4. play the piano/well

well	better	the best		badly	worse	the worst

4

Look at the chart and practice the conversation with a partner. You may supply your own choices.

A: Who's the best baseball player in the world?
B: I think _____ plays the best.
A: I don't agree. I think _____ plays better than _____. *or* I agree.

actress/act	rock singer/sing	baseball player/play	author/write
Meryl Streep	Bruce Springsteen	Eric Davis	Ken Follett
Glenda Jackson	Sting	Dave Winfield	Danielle Steele
Isabella Rossellini	George Michael	Roger Clemens	Margaret Drabble

GRAMMAR	USEFUL LANGUAGE
Mt. Everest is | higher than | Mt. McKinley. | the highest | mountain. She is | more intelligent than Joe. | the most intelligent. She writes | more clearly than Joe. | the most clearly.	Yes, I believe it is. I'm sure they're ours. Yes, you're right. I'm sorry. No problem.

1

Look at the picture. Then listen and write the name of the person.

1. Marvin   2. _____   3. _____   4. _____

5. _____   6. _____   7. _____   8. _____

2

Listen and circle the letter of the best answer.

a. I can turn it on.
b. Relax. I'll turn the oven on.
(c.) Sure. I'll turn it off.

1. a. That's my uncle, Jeff.
   b. That's my mother's brother.
   c. That's my mother.

2. a. Really? His name is Jeff.
   b. Really? I don't think so.
   c. Really? I think he looks like you.

3. a. Don't mention it.
   b. Yes, there's one across the street.
   c. Thanks a lot.

4. a. I'm the best sailor in my family.
   b. I love playing tennis.
   c. I don't play very well.

5. a. In January.
   b. In two months.
   c. In Tokyo.

6. a. I was taking a nap.
   b. I was living in New York.
   c. I wasn't here.

7. a. Yes, we were.
   b. Yes, they were.
   c. No, he wasn't.

8. a. We all pitch in.
   b. My husband makes his own bed.
   c. I don't like housework.

9. a. I'll put it away.
   b. I'll take them out.
   c. I'll put them away.

10. a. No, it's the cheapest.
    b. No, it's cheaper than his.
    c. No, it's taller than his.

11. a. The Nile.
    b. The Amazon.
    c. The Mississippi.

12. a. No, I'm sorry. It's theirs.
    b. Yes, I believe it is.
    c. They are? Yes, you're right.

STUDENT A

3 Look at the winners in these international contests. Use the charts to ask and answer questions about each contest.

A: *Sanford Smith* came in *first*. Who came in second?
B: *Alex Coe* came in second. Who came in third?
A: *Julio Borelli* came in third.

CONTEST	RESULTS		
International Opera Competition sing/beautifully	1. Sanford Smith	2. _Alex Coe_	3. Julio Borelli
Grand Auto Race Competition drive/quickly	1. _____	2. Eric Altman	3. _____
World Dance Competition dance/gracefully	1. Vera Romanova	2. _____	3. Lourdes Alonso
All Pro Swimming Competition swim/fast	1. _____	2. Flora Dale	3. _____

Check your answers with your partner. Use conversations like this:

A: Who *sings more beautifully, Julio Borelli* or *Alex Coe?*
B: *Alex Coe sings more beautifully* than *Julio Borelli.*

A: I see. Then *Sanford Smith sings* the *most beautifully.*
B: That's right.

4 Student A, start the conversation. Then listen to your partner and choose a good answer. Continue the conversation. Then try the conversation again. Choose different answers.

—What were you doing last night when I called?

—Where does he live?
—Oh, really? Like what?

—Oh, really? What was he doing there?
—Do you always do the housework in your home?

—Who does the cooking?
—Is he your mother's brother?

3

Look at the winners in these international contests. Use the chart to ask and answer questions about each contest.

CONTEST	RESULTS		
International Opera Competition sing/beautifully	1. <u>Sanford Smith</u>	2. Alex Coe	3. <u>Julio Borelli</u>
Grand Auto Race Competition drive/quickly	1. Al Moore	2. _____	3. Conrad Cooper
World Dance Competition dance/gracefully	1. _____	2. Ashley Burns	3. _____
All Pro Swimming Competition swim/fast	1. Lorraine Newkirk	2. _____	3. Linda Pells

Check your answers with a partner. Use conversations like this:

A: Who *sings more beautifully, Julio Borelli* or *Alex Coe?*
B: *Alex Coe sings more beautifully* than *Julio Borelli.*

A: I see. Then *Sanford Smith sings the most beautifully.*
B: That's right.

4

Student B, listen to your partner and choose a good answer. Continue the conversation. Then try the conversation again. Choose different answers.

—I was visiting my uncle. He's great.
—I was doing chores around the house.

—Well, I was putting away the laundry, cleaning the bathroom...
—He lives in New York now. But he was living in Japan.

—No. Everybody pitches in.
—I think he was working for an international company.

—No, he's my father's brother. I think I look like him.
—I do. But I don't do the dishes.

5

You are the president of E and A, Inc. You want to hire an assistant.
Ask three students questions and complete the chart below. Ask and
answer questions like this:

A: Do you follow directions well?
B: Yes, I do. *or* No, I don't.

	Student A	Student B	Student C
follow directions			
type			
speak English			
write reports			
use a computer			
know bookkeeping			

Now decide who you will hire. Talk about your decision with the class.

6

**Work with a partner. Ask questions about three of the activities listed
below. Write your partner's answers.**

A: Who *does* the *housework*?
B: We all pitch in.
      or *My mother and father do.*
      or *I do.*
A: Who *makes* the *beds*?
B: *My wife does.*

do/cook
do/housework
do/laundry
do/dishes
do/chores
make/beds
take out/garbage
take out/dog

Tell the class about your partner.

1

Listen to the conversation and practice with a partner.

CHUCK: Excuse me. I'd like to see *that suitcase* over there.
CLERK: Which *one*, sir?
CHUCK: *The brown canvas one.*
CLERK: *This is a* very nice *one*, sir.
CHUCK: Yes, *it is*. But *it isn't strong* enough. I need *a stronger one*.
CLERK: How about *this green one?*
CHUCK: Yes, *this is strong* enough.

Have similar conversations with a partner.

1. wallet
   black/leather
   big
   brown

2. scarves
   plaid/wool
   warm
   checked

3. briefcase
   burgundy/leather
   large
   tan

4. sweaters
   striped/wool
   soft
   plain

2

Listen to the conversation and practice with a partner. Jessica is asking Chuck about his vacation with his friends.

JESSICA: Did you enjoy your vacation?
CHUCK: No, I didn't. I was too tired to have a good time.
JESSICA: Well, did *Sam* enjoy *his* vacation?
CHUCK: No, *he* didn't. *He was* too ...

Have similar conversations with a partner.

1. Sam/worried

2. Mary/sick

3. Sue and Bob/busy

4. Christian and Tom/bored

3

Listen to the conversation and practice with a partner.

MITZI: Did you have a good time on vacation?
CHUCK: Well, I was disappointed. The *weather was* very *unpleasant*. *It was* too *unpleasant* to *have a good time*.

Have similar conversations with a partner.

1. food/bad
   eat

2. beaches/crowded
   sit on

3. city/dangerous
   go out in the evening

4. hotel/noisy
   sleep

5. ocean/rough
   swim in

6. entertainment/boring
   watch

7. pool/dirty
   go in

8. shops/expensive
   buy gifts

4

Listen to the conversation and practice with a partner. Mitzi is telling Paul about Chuck's vacation. Student A, you are Paul. Student B, you are Mitzi.

PAUL: I'm sorry Chuck didn't have a good time on vacation. What was wrong?
MITZI: Well, for one thing, the weather wasn't pleasant enough to have a good time. For another thing, _____.

Continue the conversation. Use the pictures in 3 and these words:

1. good   2. empty   3. safe   4. quiet   5. calm   6. interesting   7. clean   8. cheap

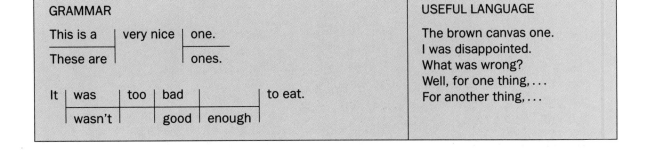

GRAMMAR						USEFUL LANGUAGE
This is a	very nice	one.				The brown canvas one.
These are		ones.				I was disappointed.
						What was wrong?
It	was	too	bad		to eat.	Well, for one thing, . . .
	wasn't		good	enough		For another thing, . . .

1

Listen to the conversation and practice with a partner.

A: *I've* made a decision. *I've* decided to look for a *job*.
B: That's terrific! *Have you done your resume* yet?
A: No, *I haven't*.
B: *Have you written* any *letters* yet?
A: No, *I haven't*.
B: *Have you looked in the want ads* yet?
A: No, not yet.
B: Well, what *have you* done?
A: Nothing yet!

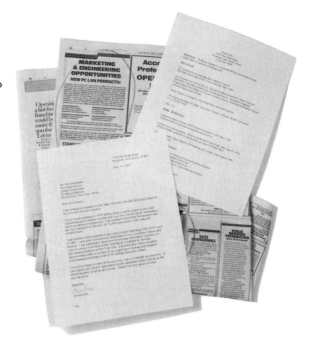

Have similar conversations with a partner.

1. Ralph
   new position
   go on any interviews
   call companies
   look in the
     classifieds

2. Pam
   college
   visit any colleges
   send for applications
   talk to other
     students

3. my parents
   new house
   see any houses
   go to real estate
     agencies
   check the
     newspapers

4. Kevin and I
   used car
   apply for a car loan
   go to car dealers
   see any nice cars

apply	applied
do	done
go	gone
see	seen
send	sent
write	written

2

Listen to the conversation and practice with a partner. A few weeks later...

B: Well, *have you* done anything yet?
A: Yes, *I've* already *done my resume*.
B: Anything else?

Continue the conversation using the items in 1.

3

Have a conversation with a partner about the following people.

A: *Jack* has already *written a resume*, but *he* hasn't *read the want ads* yet.
B: Right. And *Fred* has already *called for an appointment*, but *he hasn't written a resume* yet.

Continue...

	Already	Yet
Write a resume	Jack	Fred
Call for an appointment	Fred	Paula
Read the want ads	Yuko	Jack
Take a computer course	Vanessa	Yuko
Meet the company president	Paula	Glen
Start his job	Glen	Malcolm
Buy new clothes	Anna	Vanessa
Get a new briefcase	Malcolm	Anna

4

Listen to the conversation and practice with a partner.

BEN: *Has Nancy used* the new *word processor?*
JESS: Yes, *she has. She's* just *used it.*
BEN: Well, what *does she* think?
JESS: *It's* been here for only a few days.
BEN: Yes, but *she's used it, hasn't she?*
JESS: Yes, but *she hasn't* made up *her mind.*

Have similar conversations with a partner.

1. Heidi
   speak to
   manager

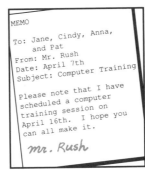

2. Mr. and Mrs. Soo
   talk to
   director

3. you and Donald
   buy
   computer

4. Corey
   see
   accountants

MEMO

To: Jane, Cindy, Anna, and Pat
From: Mr. Rush
Date: April 7th
Subject: Computer Training

Please note that I have scheduled a computer training session on April 16th. I hope you can all make it.

mr. Rush

5. the secretaries
   read
   memo

6. you
   meet
   boss

7. your husband
   hear from
   vice president

8. Charles
   try
   fax machine

buy	hear	meet	read	see	speak	talk	try
bought	heard	met	read	seen	spoken	talked	tried

GRAMMAR									USEFUL LANGUAGE
Have you	seen	her	yet?	I	have	already	seen	her.	I've made a decision.
	met				've		met		That's terrific!
Has he	talked						talked		No, not yet.
	to			He	has		to		What does she think?
					's				She hasn't made up
I haven't	seen	her	yet.						her mind.
	met								Yes, but . . .
He hasn't	talked								
	to								

47

1

Listen to the conversation and practice with a partner.

BRAD: Have you ever visited *Québec?*
RICH: No, I never have. Have you?
BRAD: Yes, I have. It's one of the most interesting *cities* I've ever seen.
RICH: Really? Well, I've gone to *Canada*, but I've never been to *Québec*.
BRAD: Maybe you'll go there someday.
RICH: I hope so.

Have similar conversations with a partner.

1. Acapulco
   resort
   Mexico

2. Ginza
   shopping area
   Tokyo

3. Waikiki
   beach
   Hawaii

4. the Parthenon
   building
   Greece

5. Naples
   seaport
   Italy

6. the Lincoln Memorial
   monument
   Washington, D.C.

7. the Louvre
   museum
   Paris

8. Stonehenge
   ruin
   England

2

Listen to the conversation and practice with a partner.

A: *Has Charles* ever been to *Los Angeles?*
B: Yes, *he has. Has Charles* ever been to *Caracas?*
A: I don't know if *he has. Has Charles* ever been to *Tokyo?*
B: No, *he hasn't.*

Have similar conversations. Student A, ask Student B about Charles.
Student B, ask Student A about Jane and Peter. Then change parts.

STUDENT A

Charles	
~~Toronto~~	the White House
Tokyo	~~Paris~~
~~Los Angeles~~	~~Lima~~

STUDENT B

Jane and Peter	
Rome	Seoul
~~Puerto Rico~~	the British Museum
~~Caracas~~	~~New York~~

3

Ask four other students in your class:

A: Have you ever | seen
                 | visited _____?
                 | been to
                 | gone to
B: Yes, I have./No, I haven't.

	Student 1	Student 2	Student 3	Student 4
London				
The Colosseum in Rome				
The pyramids in Egypt				
The Grand Canyon				
Rio de Janeiro				
Hong Kong				

4

Now talk about your findings in 3 with a partner.

Maria has *been to Miami*, but *she's* never *gone to Rio de Janeiro.*

GRAMMAR					USEFUL LANGUAGE

Have	you	ever	seen	the Grand Canyon?
I haven't			been to / gone to	the Louvre.
have		never	visited	

Yes,	I / you / we / they	have.
No,		haven't.

Yes,	he	has.
No,	she	hasn't.

USEFUL LANGUAGE

No, I never have.
Maybe you'll go there
  someday.
I hope so.
I don't know if he has.

1

Listen to the conversation and practice with a partner.

GEORGE: *Have you* been *waiting* for a long
           time?
DEBBIE: Yes, *I have. I've* been *waiting* since
           12:00.
GEORGE: It's only *12:10. You've* only been
           waiting for *ten* minutes.
DEBBIE: Is that all? It seems like forever!

Have similar conversations with a partner.

1. Sam   2. Mary   3. Mac   4. John's wife
   cook   practice   sing   work out
   10:00   11:00   6:00   8:45
   10:12   11:23   6:10   9:08

5. the boys   6. Julie and Kevin 7. Patty   8. your son
   play   paint   mow the lawn   watch MTV
   9:20   2:30   7:00   8:00
   9:35   2:45   7:18   8:45

2

Listen to the conversation and practice with a partner.

A: Who's been *waiting for ten minutes?*
B: *Debbie has.* Who's been *cooking since 10:00?*
A: *Sam has.*

**Ask a partner about who has been doing things in 1. Student A, use
these words:** sing, play, paint, watch MTV. **Student B, use these words:**
practice, work out, mow the lawn.

3

Listen to the conversation and practice with a partner.

ERIC: How long *have your parents* been *living* in *Japan?*
JANE: For *five years*.
ERIC: What *have they* been doing?
JANE: *They've* been *teaching English*.
ERIC: Oh, that sounds interesting.

Have similar conversations with a partner.

1. Kenji
   work
   Los Angeles
   three months
   teach Japanese

2. you and Sue
   stay
   Paris
   a week
   learn French

3. your children
   live
   the city
   a few weeks
   study drama

4. you
   sit
   the library
   a couple of hours
   research my paper

4

Work with a partner. Student A, look at the chart on the left. Student B, look at the chart on the right. Ask your partner the missing information about the people in your chart. Use the conversation.

A: How long *has Joe* been *living in New York?*
B: *He's* been *living in New York since 1987.* How long *have Bill and Sandy* been *living in New York?*
A: *They've* been *living in New York for 2 years.* How long . . .

SINCE	2:00
	yesterday
	December
FOR	an hour
	2 days
	6 months

STUDENT A

	Joe	Bill and Sandy
Live in New York		*2 years*
Study English		*yesterday*
Work at Chrysler Corp.	*10 months*	
Go to this school	*April*	
Use a computer		*5 years*
Play golf		*last year*

STUDENT B

	Joe	Bill and Sandy
Live in New York	*1987*	
Study English	*3 months*	
Work at Chrysler Corp.		*1976*
Go to this school		*10 weeks*
Use a computer	*last week*	
Play golf	*1 year*	

Work with a partner. Ask and answer questions like this:

A: How long have you been _____?
B: I've been _____ | for _____.
                            | since _____.

GRAMMAR					USEFUL LANGUAGE
You've She's	been living here	for	ten years. an hour. a few days.		Is that all? It seems like forever. That sounds interesting.
		since	1980. yesterday. January.		

51

1

Listen to the conversation and practice with a partner.

ADAM: Have you ever *seen a French movie?*
BRUCE: Yes, I've *seen* lots of *French movies.*
ADAM: Well, I *saw* my first one last night.
BRUCE: How did you like it?
ADAM: It was great.

Have similar conversations with a partner.

1. eat lobster

2. go to an opera

3. have a sundae

4. see a shooting star

2

Listen to the conversation and practice with a partner.

CAROL: I'm so bored.
MONICA: *So am I.*
CAROL: Do you want to see a movie tonight?
MONICA: OK. What do you want to see?
CAROL: How about *Gone With the Wind?*
MONICA: Oh, I love that movie. I haven't seen
          that in years!
CAROL: *Neither have I.* You know, I've seen it
          three times.
MONICA: *So have I.*

Later that evening . . .

CAROL: I didn't want the movie to end.
MONICA: *Neither did I.*
CAROL: I was so impressed with the acting.
MONICA: *So was I.*
CAROL: I've never seen a better movie.
MONICA: *Neither have I.*
CAROL: I want to see it again.
MONICA: *So do I.*

Now practice the conversation with the alternate form. Start like this:

CAROL: I'm so bored.
MONICA: *I am too.*
CAROL: _____

So am I.	I am too.	Neither am I.	I'm not either.
So have I.	I have too.	Neither have I.	I haven't either.
So do I.	I do too.	Neither do I.	I don't either.
So was I.	I was too.	Neither was I.	I wasn't either.
So did I.	I did too.	Neither did I.	I didn't either.

Practice the second part of the conversation in 2 so that Monica and Carol didn't like the movie. Start like this:

CAROL: I wanted the movie to end.
MONICA: *So did I.*
CAROL: _____

4

Compare the Culture Tour Packages. Work with another student and discuss the differences between the tours. Make statements like these:

A: Package A offers free admission to three museums.
B: Package B does too. Plus, Package B doesn't charge for meals.
A: Package C doesn't either. Package A doesn't give you a free bus tour.
B: You're right. Package B doesn't either.

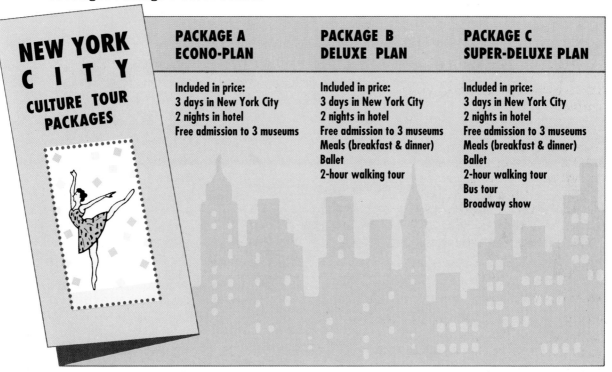

NEW YORK CITY CULTURE TOUR PACKAGES

PACKAGE A ECONO-PLAN	PACKAGE B DELUXE PLAN	PACKAGE C SUPER-DELUXE PLAN
Included in price: 3 days in New York City 2 nights in hotel Free admission to 3 museums	Included in price: 3 days in New York City 2 nights in hotel Free admission to 3 museums Meals (breakfast & dinner) Ballet 2-hour walking tour	Included in price: 3 days in New York City 2 nights in hotel Free admission to 3 museums Meals (breakfast & dinner) Ballet 2-hour walking tour Bus tour Broadway show

Work with a partner and plan your own Culture Tour Package. Then get together with another pair of students and compare your tour packages. Use a conversation like the one in 4.

GRAMMAR	USEFUL LANGUAGE
I'm bored./So am I./I am too. I've seen lots of French movies. I saw one last night. I'm not bored./Neither am I./I'm not either.	It was great. You know, I haven't seen that in years. I love that movie.

1

Look at the picture. Then listen and write T (true), F (false), or I (I don't know).

1. _F_   2. ___   3. ___   4. ___
5. ___   6. ___   7. ___   8. ___
9. ___   10. ___   11. ___   12. ___

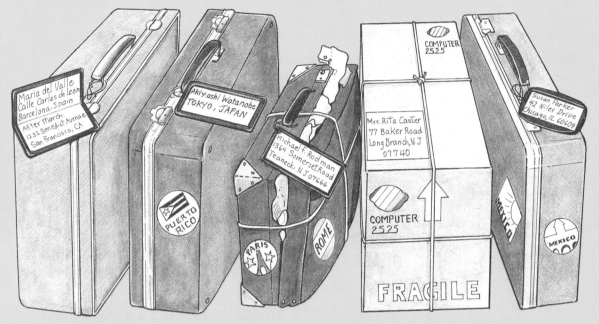

2

Listen and circle the letter of the best answer.

a. No, she was too sick to have a good time.
b. Yes, they did.
c. No, she went to the movies.

1. a. No, she hasn't seen her yet.
   b. No, they haven't.
   c. No, she hasn't spoken to him yet.

2. a. For three weeks.
   b. 11:00 o'clock.
   c. Monday.

3. a. No, never.
   b. Yes, I was.
   c. Yes, always.

4. a. So do I.
   b. So have I.
   c. So was I.

5. a. Nothing yet.
   b. No, not yet.
   c. Yes, they have.

6. a. Neither have I.
   b. Neither were we.
   c. I didn't either.

7. a. Yes. She arrived at noon and it's now 12:20.
   b. Yes. They arrived fifteen minutes ago.
   c. Yes. She arrived at 2:00 and it's now 2:10.

8. a. She hasn't seen the movie yet.
   b. She's been waiting since yesterday.
   c. She's already used her new word processor.

9. a. Yes, I've been to Los Angeles.
   b. I've always gone to California.
   c. No, he's never been to California.

10. a. Since Friday.
    b. I hope so.
    c. Yes, they will.

11. a. Have you been here?
    b. Is that all? It seems like forever.
    c. I've been watching TV.

12. a. I haven't either.
    b. No, I never have.
    c. I don't know if he has.

STUDENT A

3

A few friends are reading some postcards to you. Listen and write any information that is missing.

1. To Mike from *Amy*
    Where: *Hawaii*
    How long: since June
    Weather: *beautiful*
    Activity: visiting friends

2. To _____ from Pete and Marisa
    Where: Puerto Rico
    How long: _____
    Weather: pleasant
    Activity: _____

3. To Art from _____
    Where: _____
    How long: since Monday
    Weather: _____
    Activity: staying in bed

4. To _____ from George and Jane
    Where: London
    How long: _____
    Weather: terrible
    Activity: _____

5. To Elena from _____
    Where: _____
    How long: for three days
    Weather: _____
    Activity: taking photos

6. To _____ from Sandy
    Where: an island
    How long: _____
    Weather: cold, rainy
    Activity: _____

Check your answers with your partner. Ask about your missing information.

A: *Mike* has received a postcard from *Amy*.
B: Yes, *she's* in *Hawaii*.
A: How long *has she* been there?
B: *Since June.*
A: How has the weather been?
B: It's been *beautiful*.
A: What *has she* been doing there?
B: *She's* been *visiting friends*.

4

Student A, start the conversation. Then listen to your partner and choose a good answer. Continue the conversation. Then try the conversation again. Choose different answers.

—Did you have a good time on vacation?

—Oh, I'm sorry. Was anything else wrong?
—Where did you stay?

—Have you done anything yet?
—What does he do?

—Why not?
—Has he ever visited you and your family?

STUDENT B

3

A few friends are reading some postcards to you. Listen and write any information that is missing.

1. | To *Mike* _____ from Amy
   Where: Hawaii
   How long: *Since June* _____
   Weather: beautiful
   Activity: *visiting friends* _____

2. | To Mr. Brown from _____
   Where: _____
   How long: for two weeks
   Weather: _____
   Activity: swimming

3. | To _____ from Barry
   Where: Mexico
   How long: _____
   Weather: nice
   Activity: _____

4. | To Debbie from _____
   Where: _____
   How long: since Tuesday
   Weather: _____
   Activity: going to museums

5. | To _____ from Sam
   Where: Brazil
   How long: _____
   Weather: wonderful
   Activity: _____

6. | To Joe from _____
   Where: _____
   How long: for a week
   Weather: _____
   Activity: trying to write

Check your answers with your partner. Ask about your missing information.

A: *Mike* has received a postcard from *Amy*.
B: Yes, *she's* in *Hawaii*.
A: How long *has she* been there?
B: *Since June.*
A: How has the weather been?
B: It's been *beautiful*.
A: What *has she* been doing there?
B: *She's* been *visiting friends*.

4

Student B, listen to your partner and choose a good answer. Continue the conversation. Then try the conversation again. Choose different answers.

—No, we didn't. It was too hot to go outside.
—Yes, I did. But it wasn't long enough.

—With my cousin. He's been living in Honolulu for ten years.
—Well, I was worried. I have to look for a new job.

—Well, I've already written my resume, but I haven't sent it out yet.
—He's a doctor. He's been working in a hospital in Honolulu since 1986.

—It isn't good enough.
—No, never. But maybe he'll come here some day.

5

Ask and answer questions like this with two partners. Supply your own choices for movies, books, singers, cities, and countries. Write your choices in the chart and then check yes or no under your partners' names.

A: Have you ever *read Moby Dick?*
B: Yes, I have. *or* No, I haven't.

	Student 1		Student 2	
	YES	NO	YES	NO
_____	☐	☐	☐	☐
see (a movie)				
_____	☐	☐	☐	☐
read (a book)				
_____	☐	☐	☐	☐
hear (a singer)				
_____	☐	☐	☐	☐
visit (a city)				
_____	☐	☐	☐	☐
live in (a country)				

Now talk about your partners with the class.

A: Kenji hasn't read *Moby Dick* and neither has Paolo. Paolo has seen *Casablanca*, but Kenji hasn't.

6

Ask and answer questions with a partner. For example, you can talk about food, songs, movies, books, actors, cars, and so on.

A: *What's* the best *city* you've ever *visited?*
B: *San Francisco.*

Tell the class about your partner.

A: *San Francisco* is the best *city* _____'s ever *visited*.

Listen to the other students tell about their partners. Write the information about four students.

1

Listen to the conversation and practice with a partner.

A: Who *was* the *man* who *taught the Italian class?* I can't remember.
B: *Professor Ward was.*
A: Right. I like *him* a lot.
B: I do too.

Have similar conversations with a partner.

1. actor
    star in *New York Vice*

2. guy
    sing "Born in
    America"

3. woman
    cook on TV

4. people
    sing "Michael"

5. man
    win the election

6. women
    write the romance
    book

7. guys
    wear the red
    uniforms

8. woman
    win the tennis match

2

Listen to the conversation and practice with a partner.

A: Let's talk about *hobbies*. Which one *does* Robin like the best?
B: Hmm . . . Let me see. I guess *knitting* is the *hobby* that
     she likes the best.

Work with a partner and ask about the people in the chart.

	Joe	Mike and Sarah	Yoko	Robin	Gary
Cities	San Francisco	London	Hong Kong	Quebec	Acapulco
Hobbies	Reading	Woodworking	Playing the piano	Knitting	Collecting stamps
Sports	Tennis	Football	Golf	Skiing	Fishing
Foods	Spaghetti	Turkey	Sushi	Ice cream	Steak

3

**Talk to a partner about which city, hobby, sport, and food you like the best.
Use the conversation in 2.**

4

Listen to the conversation and practice with a partner.

A: *Which was* your favorite *high school subject?*
B: Let me see. My favorite *subject was algebra. Which was* yours?
A: Mine *was geography. Which was* your least favorite *subject?*
B: *Geometry!*

Have similar conversations with a partner about these topics: movie last year, actress now, movies this year, author, TV show, newspaper, teacher now. **Use *which* with things and *who* with persons.**

5

Listen to the conversation and practice with a partner.

MAN: *You're* from *Chicago, aren't you?*
WOMAN: Yes, *I am.*
MAN: *You go* to *Syracuse* University, *don't you?*
WOMAN: Well, yes, *I do.*
MAN: And *you* went to *Teaneck* High School, *didn't you?*
WOMAN: Yes, *I* did.
MAN: And *you* can speak *French, can't you?*
WOMAN: Uh, yes, *I can.*
MAN: *You don't* have a car, *do you?*
WOMAN: No, *I don't.*
MAN: And *you're* the *one who's* going to the Bahamas, *aren't you?*
WOMAN: Yes, *I am.*
MAN: And *you like* singing and chess.
WOMAN: Yes, *I do.* Excuse me, but where do you know *me* from?
MAN: I don't know *you.* I'm just guessing.

Have similar conversations with a partner.

1. he/Tokyo	2. they/Houston	3. she/New York	4. you and he/Florida
Keio	Northwestern	New York	Miami
the local	Wilson	Erasmus	Dade County
English	Italian	German	Spanish

GRAMMAR	USEFUL LANGUAGE
Who was the man who taught the class?	I can't remember.
Which one does she like?	I like him a lot.
Knitting is the hobby she likes.	Let's talk about...
	Where do you know me from?
	I don't know you.
	I'm just guessing.

You	are	from Chicago,	aren't	you?
	go	to Syracuse University,	don't	
	can	speak French,	can't	

You	don't	have a car,	do	you?
			don't	

1

Listen to the conversation and practice with a partner.

MS. JEFFREYS: What did you ask *Bill* to do?

MR. OKANO: I asked *him* to *open the mail* and *set up the meeting*.

Continue the conversation between Ms. Jeffreys and Mr. Okano. Use the chart below.

	Bill	Sid	Anne	Sheila	All Staff
Type the reports		X	X		
Open the mail	X				X
Go to the post office			X		
Write the report				X	
Photocopy the minutes		X			
Set up the meeting	X				
File the correspondence			X		X
Call the clients				X	
Answer the phones					X

2

Listen to the conversation and practice with a partner.

TERRY: How was your meeting with Ms. Jeffreys?

ANNA: Well, she told me to *be at work on time every day.*

TERRY: Really?

ANNA: Yes. Then she told me *not to make personal phone calls.*

TERRY: Really?

ANNA: Yes, _____.

Now look at the list and continue the conversation.

```
10 DOs AND DON'Ts OF THE WORKWELL CORPORATION

  1. Be at work on time.

  2. Don't make any personal calls.

  3. Don't take long lunch hours.

  4. Don't smoke in the work area.

  5. Dress neatly.

  6. Answer all the phones.

  7. Speak politely at all times.

  8. Don't leave the cafeteria messy.

  9. Don't eat in the office area.

 10. Don't wear blue jeans or sneakers.
```

Listen to the conversation and practice with a partner.

MR. SANCHEZ: I want to talk to you, Joan.
JOAN: Of course.
MR. SANCHEZ: I'm very happy with your work. I'm going to send you to a computer training program.
JOAN: Really?
MR. SANCHEZ: It's in Boston. You're going to stay there for two months.
JOAN: It sounds great!

Now listen to Joan's description of her meeting with Mr. Sanchez.

JOAN: My boss said he wanted to talk to me.
SAM: Oh? What happened?
JOAN: He said he was very happy with my work. Then he said he was going to send me to a computer training program. He said it was in Boston, and I was going to stay there for two months. I said it sounded great!
SAM: I think it sounds great, too. You're going to have a great time. You're really lucky! I love computers. I work with them every day and they save a lot of time. I'm taking an advanced computer course. It isn't easy, but it's fun. I know you're going to enjoy your course.

Now with a partner, take turns talking about Sam's reaction to Joan's news. Start like this:

A: Sam said he thought it sounded great, too.
B: He said she was going to have a great time.

GRAMMAR							USEFUL LANGUAGE
What did you ask him to do?							It sounds great!
I asked him to open the mail.							You're really lucky!
I want	to talk to	you.		It sounds	great.		It isn't easy, but it's fun.
He said he wanted		me.	I said	it sounded			
	I'm	happy with	your	work.			
He said	he was		my				
	It's	in Boston.					
He said	it was						

1

Listen to the conversation and practice with a partner.

A: What *are you* doing *tonight?*
B: Well, *I'm* going to *the mall*.
A: What *are you* doing there?
B: *I'm getting some clothes.*

Have similar conversations with a partner.

THINGS TO DO

√ Go to dry cleaner
  Pick up milk
√ Get gas
  Get shoes repaired

1. you and Don
   next weekend
   downtown
   do some errands

2. Fred
   on Saturday
   the city
   visit some museums

3. Joanne
   this weekend
   a sports store
   buy golf clubs

4. Linda and Dan
   this afternoon
   Saks Fifth Avenue
   go Christmas
     shopping

2

Listen to the conversation and practice with a partner.

A: What *are Tony and Dick* doing on *Saturday?*
B: *They're playing basketball.*

Work with a partner. Student A, look at the appointment book on the left. Student B, look at the appointment book on the right. Ask and answer questions to fill in the blanks. Use the conversation.

STUDENT A

SUNDAY _____
Richard — mail tickets to Kenji
Paul —
MONDAY _____
Jane —
Artie and Liz — go to the dentist
TUESDAY _____
Patrick and Norma — take Rover to the vet
Millie —
WEDNESDAY _____
Clark and Marie — cook a turkey
Estelle —
THURSDAY _____
Brenda and I —
Lenny and I — go to Montreal
FRIDAY _____
Gene —
Margie — call Mom
SATURDAY _____
Tony and Dick —
Louise and Ted — meet June and me for dinner

STUDENT B

SUNDAY _____
Richard —
Paul — study in the library
MONDAY _____
Jane — go to Boston
Artie and Liz —
TUESDAY _____
Patrick and Norma —
Millie — shop for a new dress
WEDNESDAY _____
Clark and Marie —
Estelle — get tickets for a concert
THURSDAY _____
Brenda and I — meet Nancy for lunch
Lenny and I —
FRIDAY _____
Gene — get an eye examination
Margie —
SATURDAY _____
Tony and Dick — play basketball
Louise and Ted —

3

Listen to the conversation and practice with a partner.

BRAD: Hi, *Sandy*. I have some extra theater tickets for Saturday afternoon. Are *you* free by any chance?

SANDY: No, I'm sorry, *I'm* not. *I'm* having *my apartment painted*. Why don't you call *Marie and Bob*?

Have similar conversations with a partner.

BRAD: Hi, *Marie*. I have some extra theater tickets for Saturday afternoon. Are *you and Bob* free by any chance?

MARIE: No, I'm sorry, *we're* not. _____

1. Marie and Bob
   carpet/clean
   Carl

2. Carl
   office/paint
   Gina and Rose

3. Gina and Rose
   car/repair
   Christine

4. Christine
   piano/move
   Sandy

4

Brad is telling Sandy about the people he called.

SANDY: What about *Marie and Bob*?

BRAD: *They aren't* free. *They're* having *their carpet cleaned*.

Continue the conversation with a partner. Talk about the people in 3.

5

Listen to the conversation and practice with a partner.

A: When was the last time you *had your picture taken?*

B: I had *it taken a few weeks ago*.

Work with a partner. Ask about the last time your partner had certain things done, for example, *car/wash, teeth/clean, eyes/examine, hair/cut, blood pressure/take*. Use the conversation.

GRAMMAR	USEFUL LANGUAGE
What are you doing tonight? / next weekend?	Are you free by any chance?
	Why don't you call Marie?
I'm going Christmas shopping.	When was the last time you had your picture taken?
I'm having my office painted next weekend. / my hair cut tomorrow.	

63

1

Listen to the conversation and practice with a partner.

LAWYER: What *was your sister* doing when *you left?*

MR. ALLEN: *She was writing letters.*

Have similar conversations with a partner.

1. Jack
   Mary arrive
   work

2. you
   the lights go out
   write a report

3. your mother
   the doorbell ring
   make dinner

4. you and Tom
   the storm start
   sit on the beach

5. the boys
   the accident occur
   play golf

6. Ted
   the dog bark
   take a shower

2

Listen to the conversation and practice with a partner.

A: Who was *writing letters* when *Mr. Allen left?*

B: *His sister was.*

**Have similar conversations with a partner.
Use the examples in 1.**

3

Listen to the conversation and practice with a partner.

LAWYER: What *were you* doing last night at 7:00?

VICTIM: *I* was *watching TV* in the *living room.*

LAWYER: What happened while *you were watching TV?*

VICTIM: *I heard a strange noise.*

Have similar conversations with a partner.

1. you/8:00
   read a book
   den
   see a face in the
   window

2. your daughter/8:30
   talk on the phone
   kitchen
   faint

3. your son/9:00
   take a nap
   bedroom
   have a nightmare

4. you and your
   wife/11:00
   have a snack
   dining room
   hear a crash

4

Listen to the conversation and practice with a partner.

PROSECUTOR: Where were you living five years ago?
DEFENDANT: I was living in *Miami*.
PROSECUTOR: What were you doing while you were living there?
DEFENDANT: I was *working in a restaurant*.

Have similar conversations with five people. Find out where they were living and what they were doing five years ago.

5

Patty is not having a very good day. Look at the chart and describe what happened to Patty. Start like this:

What an awful morning! When the alarm clock rang, she knocked it on the floor. While she was taking a shower, the telephone rang . . .

7:15	alarm clock rings
7:15	knocks alarm clock on the floor
7:19–7:30	takes shower
7:23	telephone rings
7:31–7:45	listens to radio
7:45	goes downstairs
7:46–7:52	makes breakfast
7:52	rips blouse
7:52	runs upstairs
7:53–7:55	changes blouse
7:55	breaks glasses
7:55	goes downstairs
7:56–8:10	eats breakfast
8:10	finishes breakfast
8:10–8:12	puts on coat
	goes to work
9:00	gets to work
	collapses

GRAMMAR	USEFUL LANGUAGE
What was your sister doing when you left? She was writing letters. What happened while you were watching TV? I heard a strange noise. What were you doing while you were living there? I was working in a restaurant. While she was taking a shower, the telephone rang.	I was. Where were you living in 1988?

1

Listen to the conversation and practice with a partner.

GRANDMA: Be careful with *that knife* or you'll hurt yourself.
BILLY: How will I hurt myself?
GRANDMA: You could *cut* yourself with *it*. I once *cut* myself very badly.

Have similar conversations with a partner.

1. matches/burn   2. broken glass/cut   3. fire/burn   4. thorns/scratch

2

Listen to the conversation and practice with a partner.

ADULT: *This cake is delicious!* Who *baked it?*
CHILD: *I* did.
ADULT: Did anybody help *you?*
CHILD: No. *I* did *it myself*.
ADULT: *You* did a great job! I used to *bake cakes*, but I don't anymore.

Have similar conversations with a partner.

1. pictures	2. room	3. photos	4. model airplane
wonderful	beautiful	lovely	perfect
draw	paint	take	build
Johnny	Billy and I	Joe and Jessica	Heather

3

Listen to the conversation and practice with a partner.

A: You used to live in *California*, didn't you?
B: Yes. I used to live in *San Francisco*.
A: Really? What part of *San Francisco* did you live in?
B: *In North Beach*. I used to walk to work. It was great.
A: Where did you work?
B: In *a restaurant*. I used to *wait on tables*.

Have similar conversations with a partner.

1. New York
   Manhattan
   In Midtown
   club/sing

2. Massachusetts
   Boston
   The North End
   restaurant/be a cook

3. California
   Los Angeles
   In Studio City
   nightclub/play the piano

4. Florida
   Miami
   Near the beach
   country club/be a lifeguard

5. Louisiana
   New Orleans
   The French Quarter
   gas station/be an auto mechanic

6. Pennsylvania
   Philadelphia
   In Center City
   law office/be a secretary

4

Practice the conversation with a partner.

A: Where did *you* use to live?
B: *I* used to live |in *Princeton*.
               |on *Nassau Street*.
               |at *122 Nassau Street*.

Work with a partner. Student A, look at the envelopes on the left. Student B, look at the envelopes on the right. Ask and answer questions to complete your envelopes. Use the conversation.

STUDENT A

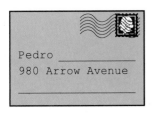

Pedro _____
980 Arrow Avenue

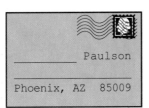

_____ Paulson

Phoenix, AZ   85009

STUDENT B

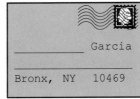

_____ Garcia

Bronx, NY   10469

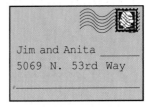

Jim and Anita _____
5069 N. 53rd Way

GRAMMAR					USEFUL LANGUAGE

GRAMMAR

I	myself	it	itself
you	yourself	we	ourselves
he	himself	you	yourselves
she	herself	they	themselves

Did she use to live in San Francisco?
No, she used to live in Los Angeles.

USEFUL LANGUAGE

Be careful with that knife.
You did a great job!
What part of town did you live in?

1

Listen and circle the letter of the best answer.

a. No, I don't.
b. Yes, we can.
c. Yes, we are.

1. a. I said it sounded great.
   b. I said I was just guessing.
   c. I said I couldn't remember.

2. a. Oh, you were?
   b. Oh, you are?
   c. Oh, you did?

3. a. They told me not to make personal phone calls.
   b. He told me to write a letter.
   c. I told them not to go to the movies.

4. a. Thanks. I took them myself.
   b. Thanks. I painted it myself.
   c. Thanks. You did it yourself.

5. a. Probably tomorrow.
   b. He had it cut a month ago.
   c. He's having it taken soon.

6. a. Mrs. Wilson did.
   b. Mrs. Wilson was.
   c. Mrs. Wilson can.

7. a. I got my office painted.
   b. We're having our carpet cleaned.
   c. She has some extra theater tickets.

8. a. He was writing a letter.
   b. He wrote a letter.
   c. He's written a letter.

9. a. I thought it sounded difficult, too.
   b. No, it didn't.
   c. You said you thought it sounded easy.

10. a. I guess reading is the hobby I like the best.
    b. Knitting is the one that she enjoys.
    c. Watching TV is a hobby I don't like.

11. a. Yours was geometry.
    b. Really? Mine was French.
    c. Really? I can speak French, too.

12. a. He told me to enjoy my new job.
    b. He's going to enjoy his new job.
    c. He said he knew I was going to enjoy my new job.

2

Look at the picture. Listen to the sentence and circle yes or no.

1. yes (no)

2. yes no

3. yes no

4. yes no

5. yes no

6. yes no

7. yes no

8. yes no

Work with a partner for Parts 3 and 4. Student A, look at this page. Student B, look at the next page.

STUDENT A

3

Listen to the four people describe themselves. Fill in the missing information.

	Ann Jones	Akiyoshi Watanabe	Jan Mason	Phillip Reese
FROM	Idaho	_____	New Jersey	_____
HIGH SCHOOL	Jackson	_____	Tenafly	_____
UNIVERSITY	_____	Rikkyo	_____	Harvard
SPEAK	_____ _____	Japanese English	_____	English Spanish
HOBBIES	knitting	_____	playing tennis	_____
NEXT VACATION	_____	Tahiti	_____	Chicago

Work with a partner. Ask and answer questions like these:

A: *Ann* is the one who's from *Idaho*, isn't *she?*
B: *Yes, she* is. *She* goes to *UCLA*, doesn't *she?*
A: *Yes, she* does.

4

Student A, start the conversation. Then listen to your partner and choose a good answer. Continue the conversation. Then try the conversation again. Choose different answers.

—You used to live in Chicago, didn't you?

—What were you doing in Washington?
—That's a beautiful area of the city, isn't it?

—Not me. The city I like the best is San Francisco.
—Really? Is it finished?

—I spent a few days there when I was driving through the United States.
—How come?

STUDENT B

3

Listen to the four people describe themselves. Fill in the missing information.

	Ann Jones	Akiyoshi Watanabe	Jan Mason	Phillip Reese
FROM	_____	Tokyo	_____	New York
HIGH SCHOOL	_____	Rikkyo	_____	Martin Luther King, Jr.
UNIVERSITY	UCLA	_____	Cornell	_____
SPEAK	German French	_____	Italian	_____
HOBBIES	_____	taking pictures	_____	watching movies
NEXT VACATION	France	_____	Rome	_____

Work with a partner. Ask and answer questions like these:

A: *Ann* is the one who's from *Idaho*, isn't *she?*
B: *Yes, she* is. *She* goes to *UCLA*, doesn't *she?*
A: *Yes, she* does.

4

Student B, listen to your partner and choose a good answer. Continue the conversation. Then try the conversation again. Choose different answers.

—No, I used to live in Washington, D.C.
—Yes, I used to live in an apartment on Lake Shore Drive.

—I was working. I was also having a house built.
—Yes, it is. I think Chicago is the city I like the best.

—Yes, but while I was having it built, I had to move away.
—When was the last time you were there?

—I'm going to do that some day.
—My company asked me to move to Montreal.

5

Work in two teams. Take a piece of paper and write sentences like these about one of the people in the picture. Do not write the name of the person.

This is a person who *was the President of the United States. He used to live in Massachusetts. He was visiting Dallas, Texas when he died.*

The teams take turns. A student on Team A reads a sentence. Students on Team B listen and try to find the person in the picture. If a student on Team B guesses the person in five seconds, Team B gets two points. If not, Team A gets a point.

1

Listen to the conversation and practice with a partner.

ANNIE: *I* really *want* to *buy a new computer*.
SAL: When *do you* expect to *buy it?*
ANNIE: Oh, not for awhile. *I* can't afford to *buy it* now.
SAL: Why *don't you* try to get a bank loan?
ANNIE: No, *I prefer* to wait.
SAL: I guess *you know* what *you want*.

Have similar conversations with a partner.

1. Joe
   need
   get
   some golf clubs

2. Jerry and Jill
   would like
   build
   a new house

3. The Boyds
   have
   lease
   a new car

4. Sylvia
   intend
   purchase
   some diamond
   earrings

With a partner, talk about something you wanted or needed to buy recently. Use the conversation.

2

Listen to the conversation and practice with a partner. Then change parts.

SAL: You look happy!
ANNIE: I am! I bought my computer!
SAL: Really? How did you do it?
ANNIE: Well, I considered asking my parents.
SAL: And?
ANNIE: _____

Continue the conversation with a partner.

1. try/save money
   myself

2. continue/work hard

3. stop/spend extra
   money

4. avoid/borrow from
   friends

Continue the conversation with a partner.

SAL: So, what did you finally do?
ANNIE: I stopped worrying. I took your advice. I got a bank loan.

3

Listen to the conversation and practice with a partner.

A: Who *minded working late at the office?*
B: *Bill* did.

Have similar conversations with a partner.

1. finish/eat dinner
   George

2. appear/be angry
   Doug and Julie

3. decide/learn Korean
   Eunice and Harvey

4. suggest/go to the
   movies/Ellen

4

Listen to the conversation and practice with a partner.

A: What do you like to do on weekends?
B: I like to read. I also like watching TV. How about you?
A: I like to play tennis. What do you hate doing?
B: I hate cleaning the house. And I hate to get up early.

**Have similar conversations with a few other students. Find out what
they like and hate doing/to do on weekends.**

5

**Work in teams. A student from Team A says a sentence with a verb
from the charts. It must be a good sentence in English. Then a student
from Team B says a different sentence. Continue until one team can't
make any more new sentences.**

Verb + to			
I *forgot* to walk the dog.			
afford	expect	intend	promise
appear	*forget*	like	try
begin	hate	love	want
continue	have	need	
decide	hope	prefer	

Verb + -ing			
I *began* studying French last month.			
avoid	enjoy	keep	prefer
begin	finish	like	stop
consider	hate	mind	suggest
continue	intend	practice	try

GRAMMAR								USEFUL LANGUAGE
I	want	to	buy a car.		I	like	cleaning	the house.	Oh, not for awhile.
	have					hate	to clean		I guess you know what
	hope					began			you want.
									You really look happy!
I	stopped	working	late.						I took your advice.
	minded								
	enjoyed								

1

Listen to the conversation and practice with a partner.

AKIKO: Excuse me, where's the *shoe* department?
MRS. KOHN: I'm sorry. I didn't hear you.
AKIKO: Could you tell me where the *shoe* department is?
MRS. KOHN: I'm not sure where it is. It's either on *3* or *4*. There's a directory over there.
AKIKO: Oh, yes. Thanks. It's on the *4th* floor.

—— BUYLENE'S ——

Jacob Whitson, Manager

BIG SALE Wednesday–Saturday

Store Directory

Accessories	1	Furniture	7
Clothing, children	3	Housewares	7
Clothing, men	6	Jewelry	1
Clothing, women	2	Shoes	4
Electronics	2	Sporting goods	2

Now practice the conversation asking about other departments.

2

Ask more questions about the store. Use the conversation in 1.

1. when/sale end   2. where/accessories   3. who/manager of store   4. when/sale begin

3

Listen to the conversation and practice with a partner.

A: Do you know what *badminton is?*
B: Yes, I do. *It's a sport.*
A: Do you know who *Toshiro Mifune is?*
B: No, I don't know who *he is.*

Ask your partner about the words in the box and other words.

What	**Where**	**When**	**Who**
sushi	Merida	Christmas	Joe Montana
rugby	the Azores	my birthday	Tom Brokaw
a wrench	Phoenix	the end of the course	Beverly Sills
a husky	Tibet	your vacation	The Rolling Stones
dominoes	Santiago		Mikhail Gorbachev
	Abu Dhabi		

4

Listen to the conversation and practice with a partner.

MRS. BARNES: May I help you?
JEFFREY: Yes, I'd like to get a gift for my *uncle*.
MRS. BARNES: Do you know what kind of gift you want?
JEFFREY: Well, no. I don't know what I want to get *him*.
MRS. BARNES: Well, what does your *uncle* need?
JEFFREY: I don't know what *he* needs.
MRS. BARNES: Does *he* have any hobbies?
JEFFREY: I don't know if *he* has any hobbies.
MRS. BARNES: Perhaps *he'd* like a *belt*. Everyone can use a *belt*. Do you know what size *he* is?
JEFFREY: Yes. He's a *36.*

Have similar conversations with a partner.

1. aunt
   blouse
   medium

2. girlfriend
   sweater
   small

3. father
   shirt
   large

4. nephew
   sweater
   small

5. cousin
   belt
   28

6. sister
   blouse
   medium

7. brother
   jacket
   38

8. sister-in-law
   ring
   5½

GRAMMAR		
Where	's	the shoe department?
	are	the toys?
Do you know		what badminton is?
		who he is?
		what kind of present you want?

USEFUL LANGUAGE
I'm sorry. I didn't hear you.
Could you tell me where...?
I'm not sure where it is.
May I help you?
Everyone can use a belt.

1

Listen to the conversation and practice with a partner.

LUCILLE: Can *you* come to *my party* next *Saturday?*
CANDICE: *I'll* have to *let you know*.
LUCILLE: I hope *you* can *come*.
CANDICE: I hope / can, too. Can / bring *my cousin* along?
LUCILLE: Sure.

Have similar conversations with a partner.

1. You and Les
   the movies
   Friday
   get back to you
   make it
   friend

2. Mr. and Mrs. Yamada
   my recital
   Sunday
   see
   be there
   daughter

3. Barry
   the meeting
   Monday
   cancel an
     appointment
   attend
   tape recorder

4. Karen
   my house
   Tuesday
   ask my Mom
   come over
   brother

2

Listen to the conversation and practice with a partner.

LUCILLE: Where *do you live?*
EDWIN: *I live* in *New York*.
LUCILLE: *You're* lucky. I wish I *lived* in *New York*, too.
EDWIN: Really? I'd rather *live* in *Florida*.

Have similar conversations with a partner.

1. Paul
   work
   Tokyo
   New York

2. you and June
   go to school
   Cambridge
   Oxford

3. your parents
   own a house
   Pennsylvania
   Los Angeles

4. Angie
   spend the summer
   Southampton
   Europe

3

Listen to the conversation and practice with a partner.

A: Where *do you* wish *you* were right now?
B: *I wish I* were *at the movies*.
A: What *do you* wish *you* were doing?
B: *I wish I* were *watching a science fiction movie*.

Work with a partner. Student A, look at the chart on the left. Student B, look at the chart on the right. A, ask B where the people in your chart wish they were and what they wish they were doing. B, ask A where the people in your chart wish they were and what they wish they were doing. Use the conversation.

STUDENT A

	Where	Doing What
Paul	in Rio de Janiero	
Al and Cal		swim
Mary	Tokyo	
Student B		

STUDENT B

	Where	Doing What
Paul		fish
Al and Cal	at the beach	
Mary		play golf
Student A		

Now talk with a partner about five things you hope you might do on your next vacation.

4

Listen to the conversation and practice with a partner.

A: I live in New York, but I wish I lived in France.
B: Me too. *or* Not me.

Have similar conversations with a partner. Talk about where you live, what you study, what you have, where you are, what you do, what you speak, and so on.

GRAMMAR	USEFUL LANGUAGE
I live | in New York. I wish | I lived Where do you | wish | you | were? I | | I | were | at the movies. I | | learned | French. Spanish. I wish I had	I hope you can come. I hope I can too. I wish I were . . . Me too. Not me.

1

Listen to the conversation and practice with a partner.

TEACHER: Do you know how many people speak *English?*
STUDENT: You mean in the world?
TEACHER: Yes.
STUDENT: I have no idea.
TEACHER: *English* is spoken by about *425* million people.
STUDENT: Wow! That's a lot.

Have similar conversations with a partner. Use the information in the chart.

Language	Million
Mandarin Chinese	806
Spanish	308
French	115
Japanese	123
Italian	63
Arabic	182
Swahili	40
Turkish	52

2

Listen to the conversation and practice with a partner.

JOSH: Which *newspaper* do you usually *read?*
MARY: I usually *read The Herald*.
JOSH: Listen to this! *The Herald* is *read* by *more than 1* million people every week.
MARY: And I'm one of them!

buy/bought
watch/watched
see/seen
ride/ridden
fly/flown
take/taken
eat/eaten

Have similar conversations with a partner.

1. magazine
   buy
   Newstime
   approximately/3

2. TV program
   watch
   Family Fight
   about/30

3. soap opera
   see
   Young Hospital
   almost/10

4. airline
   fly
   Pan-World
   just about/7

5. train
   take
   the West Railroad
   nearly/2

6. highway
   take
   Route 4W
   roughly/a quarter

7. ice cream
   eat
   Len and Barry's
   more than/a half

8. bus
   ride
   Whitehound
   close to/1

3

Work with a partner. Say where certain languages are spoken in the world. You can use the list of languages from 1.

A: A lot of people speak *Italian*. Do you know where it's spoken?

B: It's spoken in *Italy, Switzerland, San Marino, . . .*

4

Listen to the conversation and practice with a partner.

A: Where is the world's *largest dome* found?

B: It's found in *the United States*.

A: What's it called?

B: It's called the *Louisiana Superdome*.

Have similar conversations with a partner.

1. large
   pyramid
   Mexico
   Quetzacoatl

2. long
   subway tunnel
   the Soviet Union
   Moscow Metro

3. big
   shopping center
   Canada
   West Edmonton Mall

4. tall
   tower
   Canada
   CN Tower

5. high
   building
   the United States
   Sears Tower

6. wide
   bridge
   Australia
   Sydney Harbour
    Bridge

GRAMMAR	USEFUL LANGUAGE
A lot of people read *The Herald*. *The Herald* is read by a lot of people. A lot of people speak Italian. Do you know where it's spoken? It's spoken in Italy, Switzerland...	I have no idea. Wow! That's a lot! Listen to this! And I'm one of them!

1

Listen to the conversation and practice with a partner.

POLICE OFFICER: Ladies and gentlemen. The
                   Cope Diamond was stolen
                   last night.
REPORTER: Do you know who *stole it?*
POLICE OFFICER: We don't know who did it.
                   But we have a lot of clues.
REPORTER: Did they *steal anything*
                   else?
POLICE OFFICER: No, *nothing* else.

Have similar conversations with a partner.

1. gray pearls of India
   take
   anything/nothing

2. empress
   shoot
   anybody/nobody

3. count and countess
   rob
   anyone/no one

4. Mrs. Ransom
   kidnap
   anybody/nobody

2

Listen to the quiz program and practice with a partner.

TV HOST: Which category would you like?
CONTESTANT: How about *literature?*
TV HOST: OK. Here's your question. You
               have ten seconds. Who *wrote*
               Hamlet?
CONTESTANT: *Hamlet* was *written* by
               Shakespeare.

Conduct a similar quiz program with a partner.

A. Literature wrote/ written	B. Inventions invented/ invented	C. Discoveries discovered/ discovered
1. *The Mouse Trap*	1. television	1. penicillin
2. *A Christmas Carol*	2. the hot air balloon	2. the New World
3. *Ulysses*	3. the camera	3. the conditioned reflex
4. *100 Years of Solitude*	4. dynamite	4. Labrador
5. *Tom Sawyer*	5. the airplane	5. Brazil

Listen to the conversation and practice with a partner.

A: When *was The Sound of Music made?*
B: Give me a minute. Let me see... *It was made in 1965.*

Have similar conversations with a partner. Use the chart.

Born		Made		Completed
Margaret Thatcher	1925	*Crocodile Dundee*	1986	The pyramids in Egypt about 2800 B.C.
Diane Sawyer	1945	*E.T.*	1982	The Colosseum in Rome about 80 A.D.
Sylvester Stallone	1949	*Star Wars*	1977	The Taj Mahal in India 1650 A.D.
Princess Diana of Wales	1961	*The Godfather*	1972	The Great Wall of China about 228 B.C.
Jesse Jackson	1941	*The Sound of Music*	1965	Westminster Abbey in London 1065 A.D.

4

Work with a partner. Make a chart similar to the one in 3. You may choose different categories if you wish. Then, work with another pair and ask and answer each other's questions.

Answers for 2:
A.   1. Agatha Christie   2. Charles Dickens   3. James Joyce
    4. Gabriel García Márquez   5. Mark Twain
B.   1. John Logie Baird   2. the Montgolfier Brothers   3. George Eastman
    4. Alfred Nobel   5. The Wright Brothers
C.   1. Alexander Fleming   2. Christopher Columbus   3. Ivan Pavlov
    4. Leif Ericson   5. Pedro Cabral

GRAMMAR	USEFUL LANGUAGE
The Cope Diamond was stolen. Do you know who stole it? Did they steal anything else?	We don't know who did it. But we have a lot of clues. No, nothing else. Here's your question. Give me a minute.

1

Listen and circle the letter of the best answer.

(a.) It was written by Margaret Mitchell.
b. It was written in 1936.
c. I wrote it.

1. a. I hope he can come.
   b. I wish I lived in New York.
   c. I hope I can be there.

2. a. I'm not sure where it is.
   b. I don't know what it is.
   c. I'm not sure when it is.

3. a. No, I don't know.
   b. Yes, it's on the first floor.
   c. Yes, can you tell me when the store closes?

4. a. I wish I were at the movies.
   b. I wish I lived there, too.
   c. I'd rather live in San Francisco.

5. a. I wish I were in Puerto Rico.
   b. I wish I were swimming.
   c. I wish I were at the movies.

6. a. That's a lot!
   b. I have no idea.
   c. Listen to this!

7. a. It's found in Alaska.
   b. I found it!
   c. It's called Mt. McKinley.

8. a. I am.
   b. I can.
   c. He appeared to be angry.

9. a. Me too.
   b. I am, too.
   c. I did, too.

10. a. I went.
    b. I was.
    c. My parents did.

11. a. Do you know what he needs?
    b. Would you like to see it?
    c. Do you know where he is?

12. a. You don't know who stole it.
    b. Do you know who stole them?
    c. Do you know who stole it?

2

Look at the picture. Listen to the sentence and circle a, b, or c.

1. (a) b c

2. a b c

3. a b c

4. a b c

5. a b c

6. a b c

7. a b c

8. a b c

STUDENT A

3

Four people are buying presents. Listen to their conversations. Write any information that is missing.

1. Bill
   for: _father_
   hobbies: playing golf
   present: _golf shoes_
   size: ten
   color: _green_

2. Alan and Jim
   for: _____
   hobbies: skiing
   present: _____
   size: small
   color: _____

3. Rhoda
   for: mother
   hobbies: _____
   present: gloves
   size: _____
   color: purple

4. Ginny and Kim
   for: teacher
   hobbies: _____
   present: sweater
   size: _____
   color: red

Check your answers with your partner. Start like this:

A: Can you tell me who *Bill is* buying a present for?
B: *He is* buying a present for *his father*. Do you know if *his father* has any hobbies?
A: Yes, *he* enjoys *playing golf.* Do you know what present *Bill wants* to buy?
B: Yes, *he wants* to buy *golf shoes.* Can you tell me what size *shoes he* wears?
A: Yes, *he wears a ten.* Do you know what *his* favorite color is?
B: Yes, *his* favorite color is *green.*

4

Student A, start the conversation. Then listen to your partner and choose a good answer. Continue the conversation. Then try the conversation again. Choose different answers.

—What would you enjoy doing on Sunday?

—I hate working at home.
—Good. Would you mind seeing *The Blue Diamond?*

—I wish you didn't always have to work on the weekends.
—It's about a robbery. Some jewels are stolen from a museum.

—Well, maybe if you work hard this week...
—Sure. That's OK with me.

STUDENT B

3

Four people are buying presents. Listen to their conversations. Write any information that is missing.

1. Bill
   for: father
   hobbies: _playing golf_
   present: golf shoes
   size: _ten_
   color: green

2. Alan and Jim
   for: sister
   hobbies: _____
   present: a hat
   size: _____
   color: yellow

3. Rhoda
   for: _____
   hobbies: gardening
   present: _____
   size: 6 1/2
   color: _____

4. Ginny and Kim
   for: _____
   hobbies: tennis
   present: _____
   size: large
   color: _____

Check your answers with your partner. Start like this:

A: Can you tell me who *Bill is* buying a present for?

B: *He is* buying a present for *his father*. Do you know if *his father* has any hobbies?

A: Yes, *he* enjoys *playing golf*. Do you know what present *Bill wants* to buy?

B: Yes, *he wants* to buy *golf shoes*. Can you tell me what size *shoes he wears?*

A: Yes, *he wears a ten*. Do you know what *his* favorite color is?

B: Yes, *his* favorite color is *green*.

4

Student B, listen to your partner and choose a good answer. Continue the conversation. Then try the conversation again. Choose different answers.

—I'd love to go to the movies.
—Nothing. I intend to work on Sunday.

—So do I. But I have to write a report.
—No. Do you know what it's about?

—Me too. Everyone can use a day off.
—Sounds great! I hope we can go in the afternoon.

—If we get home early, we can finish painting the bedroom.
—Maybe we can go somewhere next weekend. I'll have to let you know.

5

Work in two teams. Take a piece of paper and write five WHERE questions and answers and five WHEN questions and answers like these:

WHERE

Where is Urdu spoken?
Do you know where the Andes are found?
Can you guess where _____ was born?
               (name of student)

It is spoken in Pakistan.
They are found in South America.
_____ was born in _____.
(name of student)

WHEN

When were the Pyramids built?
Can you tell me when Christmas is celebrated?
Can you guess when _____ was born?
               (name of student)

They were built about 2800 B.C.
It is celebrated on December 25th.
_____ was born in _____.
(name of student)

The teams take turns. A student on Team A reads a WHERE question. Students on Team B listen and try to say the answer. If a student on Team B says the answer in five seconds, Team B gets two points. If not, Team A gets a point. On the next turn, a student on Team B reads a WHEN question. Continue until one team scores ten points.

6

Ask and answer questions like these with three partners. Write their answers.

A: Where do you wish you were right now?
B: I wish I were *in Spain*.
A: What do you wish you were doing?
B: I wish I were *sitting on a beach*.

	Student 1	Student 2	Student 3
Where			
What			

Tell the class about your partners.

A: Pedro wishes he were in Spain right now. He wishes he were sitting on a beach. Annabelle wishes _____.

Word and Phrase List

This word and phrase list contains the words and phrases found in *On Course 2* Student Book. The list may not contain all of the words used in the accompanying cassette. The number next to each word indicates what unit it occurs in for the first time.

A

a couple of *19*
a few *3*
a little *2*
a lot (of) *9*
about *9*
above *10*
accident *24*
accountant *17*
accurate *14*
across from *10*
act *15*
actor *21*
actress *15*
admission *20*
advance *22*
advice *26*
aerobics *5*
afford *26*
afloat *7*
after *5*
afternoon *6*
again *20*
against *10*
agency *17*
ago *11*
agree *14*
alarm clock *24*
algebra *21*
all *6*
almost *29*
along *28*
already *17*
always *1*
and *1*
angry *26*
animal *12*
anniversary *4*
annual *14*
another *6*
answer (v) *1*
answering machine *1*
any *5*
anybody *25*
anymore *25*
anyone *30*
anything *5*
apartment *5*
appear *26*
application *17*

apply for *17*
appointment *28*
approximately *29*
arrive *6*
as soon as *12*
ask *22*
aspirin *3*
at *1*
attend *28*
aunt *11*
author *15*
auto mechanic *25*
avoid *26*
awful *3*
awhile *26*

B

backache *3*
bad *3*
badly *14*
badminton *27*
bag *9*
bake *4*
balance *S2*
ball *7*
bank loan *26*
bark (v) *24*
baseball *7*
basketball *23*
bath *5*
bathroom *5*
be *1*
be able to *7*
be ready *8*
beach *S1*
beautiful *10*
because *1*
bed *3*
bedroom *10*
beer *9*
begin *2*
believe *15*
belt *27*
best *15*
better *3*
between *S2*
big *15*
bike *1*
birthday *4*
black *16*

bleed *3*
block (n) *13*
blouse *24*
boat *6*
book *4*
bookcase *10*
bored *16*
borrow *26*
boss *17*
bottle *9*
bowl *7*
box *9*
boy *13*
bracelet *4*
brand new *10*
break *3*
breakfast *12*
bridal shower *9*
bridge *29*
briefcase *15*
bring *4*
brother *1*
brown *16*
build *25*
building *6*
burgundy *16*
burn *25*
bury *11*
bus *1*
busy *4*
but *1*
butter *9*
buy *1*
by *1*
by any chance *23*

C

cabinet *10*
cake *4*
call *3*
call up *12*
calm *16*
can *9*
can (v) *2*
cancel *28*
candy *4*
canvas *16*
car *2*
cards *7*
careful *14*

carefully *14*
careless *14*
carelessly *14*
carpet *23*
cat *12*
category *30*
cereal *9*
certain *5*
certainly *4*
change (v) *24*
charge *20*
cheap *16*
check (v) *17*
checked *16*
cheese *9*
chess *21*
chicken *9*
child (children) *2*
chocolate *4*
chore *12*
Christmas *4*
city *1*
class *5*
classified *17*
clean *16*
clean (v) *5*
clean out *12*
clear *14*
clinic *3*
close to *29*
closet *10*
clothes *4*
club *5*
coat *24*
coffee *9*
cold (n) *S1*
collapse *24*
collect *21*
college *17*
color *S6*
company *17*
complain *3*
concert *11*
consider *26*
container *9*
continent *15*
continue *26*
cook *25*
cook (v) *4*
cookie *9*

corner 10
cotton 4
cough medicine S1
could 7
counter 12
country club 25
course 8
cousin 13
cracker 9
crash 24
cream cheese 9
crowded 16
cruise 6
cuff link 4
cup 9
cut (n) 3

D

dangerous 16
database 2
daughter 2
day 3
day off S6
dealer 17
decide 17
decision 12
deep 15
delicious 6
den 10
dentist S1
depart 6
department 27
develop 8
diamond 4
diary 6
dictionary 4
dining room 24
dinner 5
direction 14
director 17
directory 27
dirty 16
disappoint 16
dish 12
dishwasher 12
do 1
doctor S1
documentary 11
dog 4
dome 29
door 10
doorbell 24
downstairs 10
downtown 23
draw 25
dress (n) 4
dresser 10
drive 1

driver's license 2
drugstore S1
dry (adj.) 9
during 5
dust (v) 12

E

each 10
early 26
earring 4
easy 22
eat 1
eat out 1
either 10
election 21
electronic 2
emergency room 3
empress 30
empty 16
end 10
end (v) 20
enjoy 11
enough 10
entertainment 16
errand 13
evening 1
everyone 27
everything 6
excellent 2
Excuse me. 4
exercise 5
exhausted S1
expect 26
expensive 16
extra 23
eye 3

F

face 24
fail 8
faint 24
fall asleep 5
family 11
famous 6
fast 14
father 11
favor 12
favorite 21
fax machine 2
feed 14
feel 3
ferry 6
fever 3
film 8
finally 26
find 4
fine 2
finish 24

fire (n) 25
first 5
fish 28
fish (v) 21
fit 10
fix 5
floor 24
flower 4
flu 3
fly (v) 1
follow 14
food 12
foot 7
football 7
forever 19
forget 12
form 14
free 20
friend 1
from 6
full day 5
fun 7
future 14

G

garbage 12
garden 7
gas station 25
geographical 15
geography 21
geometry 21
get 4
get along (with) 13
get back to . . . 28
get off 13
get on 13
get ready 5
gift 16
give 4
glad 14
glass 25
glasses (eye) 24
glove 4
go 1
go ahead 3
go back 5
go on (an interview) 17
go out 5
gold 4
golf 7
golf club 23
good 2
graduation 4
gram 9
grandfather 13
grandmother 13
great 2

green 16
groan 3
guess 2
guy 21
gym 1

H

hair 23
haircut 5
half 9
half-full 9
half-gallon 9
hand (v) 4
handkerchief 4
hang up 12
happy 13
hard 14
hate (v) 26
have 2
have to 3
he 1
headache 3
health 5
hear 8
heart 4
hello 12
help 27
here 1
hi 1
high 15
high school 21
his 1
hit 7
hobby 21
home 1
hope 26
hot 5
hotel 16
hour 6
house 8
household 12
housework 12
how 6
How about . . . ? 10
How come? 14
How long . . . ? 19
how many . . . ? 9
how much . . . ? 9
huge 10
hurt 3
husband 1

I

I 1
ice cream 21
ice skate 7
idea 4
immediately 2

impolite 14
important 3
impress 20
in 25
inaccurate 14
intelligent 15
intend to S6
interesting 16
international S3
interview 17
iron (n) 12
island 15
it 7

J

jacket 27
jewelry 4
job 8
juice 9
just 10

K

keep 7
kidnap 30
kid (n) 1
kitchen 10
knife 25
knit 14
knitter 14
knock 24
know 28

L

Ladies and gentlemen.
    30
ladies room 27
lake 15
lamp 10
language 2
large 9
last 6
late 1
laundry 5
laundry room 10
law office 25
lawn 19
lean 17
learn 19
lease (v) 26
least 21
leather 4
leave (left) 1
lecture 1
leftover 12
less 15
lesson 14
let 28
let out 12

letter 8
library 1
lifeguard 25
lift 5
light (n) 24
like 6
like (v) 7
lion 14
liquid 9
list 9
listen 12
liter 9
literature 30
live (v) 10
living room 10
lobster 20
local 21
long 15
look for 17
look like 13
lose 8
lots 6
love 11
lovely 25
lucky 22
luggage 11
lunch 12

M

magazine 12
mail (n) 22
make 4
make up one's mind
    17
mall 11
man 13
manager 17
marathon 5
match (n) 25
may 3
maybe 13
me 2
meal 6
measure 9
medicine S1
medium 27
meet 5
meeting 3
memo 14
message 1
might 8
mile 5
million 29
mind (v) 12
minute 2
mirror 10
miss 1
Miss 2

model airplane 25
money 26
month 11
monument 18
more 2
morning S1
most 11
mother 11
mother-in-law 13
mountain 15
move 5
movie 1
mow 19
Mr. 2
Mrs. 2
Ms. 2
MTV 19
museum 18
music 5
my 1
myself 25

N

nap 11
nasal spray 3
near 25
nearly 29
necklace 4
need 8
nephew 13
nervous 14
never 1
new 10
news 14
newspaper 4
next 5
nice 10
niece 13
night 16
nightclub 25
nightmare 24
no 1
no one 30
nobody S1
noisy 16
none 9
north 13
nose 3
not 5
nothing 17
now 1

O

occur 24
ocean 6
of course 6
offer (v) 20
office 1

often 1
oh 1
Oh, no! 3
OK 4
on 1
on the left/right 10
on time 22
once 25
one 2
only 9
open 22
opera 11
operation 8
opposite 10
or 15
other 1
Ouch! 3
ounce 9
our 12
oven 12
over there 16
own 2

P

package 20
painful 3
paint (v) 5
paper 19
parent 1
park (n) 11
part 25
party 9
pasta 9
patio 10
pearl 4
people 13
perfect 25
perhaps 27
personal 22
phone call 1
photo 25
piano 14
pick up 9
picnic 8
picture 8
piece 9
pill 3
pint 9
pitch in S3
place 10
plaid 16
plain 16
plane 6
plant (n) 10
plastic 4
play (v) 5
player 14
please 3

plus *20*
pocketbook *15*
poison *11*
politely *14*
pool *16*
poor *14*
poorly *14*
populate *15*
position *17*
post office *13*
potato chips *9*
pots and pans *10*
pound *9*
practice *19*
prefer *26*
present (n) *4*
president *17*
Pretty good. *9*
probably *3*
program *22*
promise (v) *26*
purchase *26*
put away *12*
put in *S2*
put on *24*
pyramid *29*

Q

quart *9*
question *2*
quick *14*
quickly *14*
quiet *16*

R

racquetball *5*
radio *24*
rain (v) *8*
raincoat *15*
read *4*
reader *4*
real estate *17*
really *1*
receive *S4*
reception *9*
recital *28*
record (v) *11*
red *4*
refrigerator *S2*
relax *6*
remember *21*
rent (v) *6*
repair (v) *23*
report (n) *14*
research (v) *19*
resort *18*
restaurant *24*
resume *S1*

ride *1*
right away *2*
Right. *9*
ring *4*
ring (v) *24*
rip *24*
river *15*
rock singer *15*
rocking chair *10*
roller skate *7*
romance *21*
roof *5*
room *25*
roommate *12*
rose *4*
rough *16*
roughly *29*
ruby *4*
ruin *18*
run *5*
runner *14*
rob *30*

S

safe (adj.) *16*
sail (v) *6*
sailor *S3*
salad *9*
sale *27*
sauce *9*
save *22*
say *22*
scarf *4*
school *1*
scratch (v) *25*
scream (v) *3*
seaport *18*
seat *15*
second *30*
secretary *25*
see *1*
sell *8*
send *4*
serious *3*
set up *22*
sheet *12*
shirt *12*
shoe *27*
shoot *30*
shooting star *20*
shop *16*
shop (v) *12*
shopping area *18*
shopping bag *15*
shopping center *29*
should *3*
show (v) *4*
show up *13*

shower *12*
sick *3*
side *10*
sightsee *6*
silk *4*
silver *4*
since *19*
sing *14*
sink (n) *10*
sir *16*
sister *2*
sit *16*
size *27*
ski jumping *7*
skill *14*
sleep *1*
slow *14*
small *9*
snake *14*
so *9*
soda *9*
soft *16*
softball *7*
some *3*
someday *18*
sometimes *1*
son *2*
sore *3*
sorry *3*
spaghetti *21*
speak *2*
spend *14*
sport *7*
sporting goods *23*
spring *S1*
stamp (n) *21*
star (v) *21*
start (v) *15*
stay *2*
steak *21*
steal *30*
still *8*
stomachache *3*
stop *3*
store *5*
storm *24*
straight home *5*
straighten up *12*
strange *24*
striped *16*
strong *16*
student *17*
study *1*
stuffy *3*
subject *21*
subway tunnel *29*
sugar *9*
suggest *26*

suitcase *16*
summer *S1*
sundae *20*
sunglasses *4*
supermarket *1*
sure *4*
sushi *21*
sweater *4*
swim *5*
swimmer *14*

T

table *25*
take *1*
take off *8*
take out *12*
talk *17*
tall *15*
tan *16*
tape recorder *28*
teach *19*
telephone *1*
tell *2*
tennis *7*
tennis match *21*
terrible *3*
terrific *17*
than *15*
Thank you. *4*
Thanks. *S1*
that *3*
That's easy. *9*
the *1*
theater *23*
them *4*
then *3*
there *6*
these *3*
they *1*
thing *5*
think *5*
this *3*
thorn *25*
those *4*
throat *3*
through *S2*
throw out *12*
ticket *23*
tie (n) *4*
time *3*
tired *5*
to *1*
today *1*
tomato *9*
tomorrow *2*
tonight *7*
too *7*
toothache *3*

tour *20*
towel *12*
tower *29*
toy *12*
train *1*
training *22*
trip (n) *S1*
trivia *15*
try *14*
tuna fish *9*
turkey *21*
turn off *12*
turn on *5*
TV *4*
twins *4*
type *2*
typewriter *2*

U
uncle *11*
under *10*
understand *11*
uniform *21*
university *21*
unless *8*
unpleasant *16*
upstairs *10*
us *5*
use (v) *2*
used car *17*
used to *25*
usually *1*

V
vacation *6*
vacuum *12*
Valentine's Day *4*
VCR *5*
very *25*
vice president *17*
video *5*
videocassette *4*
visit (v) *1*

W
wait *4*
wait for *19*
wait on *25*
wake up *5*
walk (v) *1*
wall *10*
want *22*
want ad *17*
warm *16*
was *6*
wash *5*
wash off *12*
waste time *5*

watch *4*
watch (v) *5*
waterfall *15*
way *1*
we *2*
weak point *14*
weather *8*
week *5*
weekend *S1*
weight *5*
well *7*
Well, ... *1*
What about ... *14*
what *1*
when *2*
where *S4*
which *16*
while *24*
whisper *3*
who *1*
why *14*
wide *29*
wife *1*
win *21*
window *10*
wine *9*
wish (v) *28*
with *13*
woman *13*
wonder *8*
wonderful *2*
woodworking *21*
wool *4*
word *2*
word processor *2*
work (n) *1*
work evaluation *14*
work out (v) *5*
world *15*
worry *12*
worst *15*
would *4*
would like *26*
would rather *28*
Wow! *29*
write *8*
wrong *13*

Y
year *7*
yell *3*
yes *1*
yesterday *11*
yet *8*
yogurt *9*
You know, ... *20*
you *1*
your *1*